THE ORIGINAL SLOW COOKER

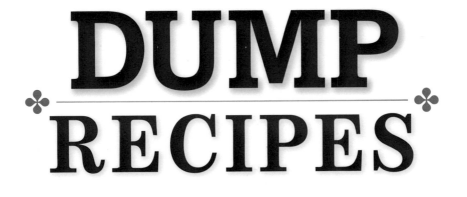

DUMP RECIPES

Publications International, Ltd.

Pictured on the front cover: Ranch Stew *(page 108)*.

Pictured on the back cover *(left to right):* Chicken and Butternut Squash *(page 74)*, Corn and Two Bean Chili *(page 112)* and Pollo Ranchero (Country Chicken) *(page 58)*.

ISBN: 978-1-4508-9774-7

Library of Congress Control Number: 2014950371

Manufactured in China.

8 7 6 5 4 3 2 1

Publications International, Ltd.

TABLE OF ✿CONTENTS✿

✿ SLOW COOKING 101 ✿

CROCK-POT® Slow Cooker Sizes

Smaller **CROCK-POT®** slow cookers—such as 1- to 3½-quart models—are the perfect size for cooking for singles, a couple or empty-nesters (and also for serving dips).

While medium-size **CROCK-POT®** slow cookers (those holding somewhere between 3 quarts and 5 quarts) will easily cook enough food at a time to feed a small family, they're also convenient for holiday side dishes or appetizers.

Large **CROCK-POT®** slow cookers are great for large family dinners, holiday entertaining and potluck suppers. A 6- to 7-quart model is ideal if you like to make meals in advance, or have dinner tonight and store leftovers for another day.

Types of CROCK-POT® Slow Cookers

Current **CROCK-POT®** slow cookers come equipped with many different features and benefits, from auto cook programs to oven-safe stoneware to timed programming. Visit **www.crock-pot.com** to find the **CROCK-POT®** slow cooker that best suits your needs.

How you plan to use a **CROCK-POT®** slow cooker may affect the model you choose to purchase. For everyday cooking, choose a size large enough to serve your family. If you plan to use the **CROCK-POT®** slow cooker primarily for entertaining, choose one of the larger sizes. Basic **CROCK-POT®** slow cookers can hold as little as 16 ounces or as much as 7 quarts. The smallest sizes are great for keeping dips warm on a buffet, while the larger sizes can more readily fit large quantities of food and larger roasts.

Cooking, Stirring and Food Safety

CROCK-POT® slow cookers are safe to leave unattended. The outer heating base may get hot as it cooks, but it should not pose a fire hazard. The heating element in the heating base functions at a low wattage and is safe for your countertops.

Your **CROCK-POT®** slow cooker should be filled about one-half to three-fourths

full for most recipes unless otherwise instructed. Lean meats such as chicken or pork tenderloin will cook faster than meats with more connective tissue and fat such as beef chuck or pork shoulder. Bone-in meats will take longer than boneless cuts. Typical **CROCK-POT®** slow cooker dishes take approximately 7 to 8 hours to reach the simmer point on LOW and about 3 to 4 hours on HIGH. Once the vegetables and meat start to simmer and braise, their flavors will fully blend and meat will become fall-off-the-bone tender.

According to the USDA, all bacteria are killed at a temperature of 165°F. It's important to follow the recommended cooking times and not to open the lid often, especially early in the cooking process when heat is building up inside the unit. If you need to open the lid to check on your food or are adding additional ingredients, remember to allow additional cooking time if necessary to ensure food is cooked through and tender.

Large **CROCK-POT®** slow cookers, the 6- to 7-quart sizes, may benefit from a quick stir halfway through cook time to help distribute heat and promote even cooking. It's usually unnecessary to stir at all, as even ½ cup liquid will help to distribute heat and the stoneware is the perfect medium for holding food at an even temperature throughout the cooking process.

Oven-Safe

All **CROCK-POT®** slow cooker removable stoneware inserts may (without their lids) be used safely in ovens at up to 400°F. Also, all **CROCK-POT®** slow cookers are microwavable without their lids. If you own another brand slow cooker, please refer to your owner's manual for specific stoneware cooking medium tolerances.

Frozen Food

Frozen food can be successfully cooked in a **CROCK-POT®** slow cooker; however, it will require longer cooking time than the same recipe made with fresh food. It's almost always preferable to thaw frozen food prior to placing it in the **CROCK-POT®** slow cooker. Using an instant-read thermometer is recommended to ensure meat is fully cooked through.

Pasta and Rice

If you're converting a recipe that calls for uncooked pasta, cook the pasta on the stovetop just until slightly tender before adding to the **CROCK-POT®** slow cooker. If you are converting a recipe that calls for cooked rice, stir in raw rice with other ingredients; add ¼ cup extra liquid per ¼ cup of raw rice.

Beans

Beans must be softened completely before combining with sugar and/or acidic foods. Sugar and acid have a hardening effect on beans and will prevent softening. Fully cooked canned beans may be used as a substitute for dried beans.

page 28

Vegetables

Root vegetables often cook more slowly than meat. Cut vegetables accordingly to cook at the same rate as meat—large or small or lean versus marbled—and place near the sides or bottom of the stoneware to facilitate cooking.

Herbs

Fresh herbs add flavor and color when added at the end of the cooking cycle; if added at the beginning, many fresh herbs' flavor will dissipate over long cook times.

Ground and/or dried herbs and spices work well in slow cooking and may be added at the beginning of cook time. For dishes with shorter cook times, hearty fresh herbs such as rosemary and thyme hold up well. The flavor power of all herbs and spices can vary greatly depending on their particular strength and shelf life. Use chili powders and garlic powder sparingly, as these can sometimes intensify over the long cook times. Always taste the finished dish and correct seasonings including salt and pepper.

Liquids

It's not necessary to use more than 1/2 to 1 cup liquid in most instances since juices in meats and vegetables are retained more in slow cooking than in conventional cooking. Excess liquid can be cooked down and concentrated after slow cooking on the stovetop or by removing meat and vegetables from stoneware, stirring in one of the following thickeners and setting the slow cooker to HIGH. Cover; cook on HIGH for approximately 15 minutes or until juices are thickened.

Flour: All-purpose flour is often used to thicken soups or stews. Stir cold water into the flour in a small bowl until smooth. With the **CROCK-POT**® slow cooker on HIGH, whisk the flour mixture into the liquid in the **CROCK-POT**® slow cooker. Cover; cook on HIGH 15 minutes or until the mixture is thickened.

Cornstarch: Cornstarch gives sauces a clear, shiny appearance; it's used most often for sweet dessert sauces and stir-fry sauces. Stir cold water into the cornstarch in a small bowl until the cornstarch dissolves. Quickly stir this mixture into the liquid in the **CROCK-POT**® slow cooker; the sauce will thicken as soon as the liquid simmers. Cornstarch breaks down with too much heat, so never add it at the beginning of the slow cooking process and turn off the heat as soon as the sauce thickens.

Arrowroot: Arrowroot (or arrowroot flour) comes from the root of a tropical plant that is dried and ground to a powder; it produces a thick clear sauce. Those who are allergic to wheat often use it in place of flour. Place arrowroot in a small bowl or cup and stir in cold water until the mixture is smooth. Quickly stir this mixture into the liquid in the **CROCK-POT**® slow cooker. Arrowroot thickens below the boiling point, so it even works well in a **CROCK-POT**® slow cooker on LOW. Too much stirring can break down an arrowroot mixture.

Tapioca: Tapioca is a starchy substance extracted from the root of the cassava plant. Its greatest advantage is that it withstands long cooking, making it an ideal choice for slow cooking. Add it at the beginning of cooking and you'll get a clear thickened sauce in the finished dish. Dishes using tapioca as a thickener are best cooked on the LOW setting; tapioca may become stringy when boiled for a long time.

Milk

Milk, cream and sour cream break down during extended cooking. When possible, add them during the last 15 to 30 minutes of cooking, until just heated through. Condensed soups may be substituted for milk and can cook for extended times.

Fish

Fish is delicate and should be stirred in gently during the last 15 to 30 minutes of cooking time. Cover and cook just until cooked through and serve immediately.

page 180

Baked Goods

If you wish to prepare bread, cakes or pudding cakes in a **CROCK-POT**® slow cooker, you may want to purchase a covered, vented metal cake pan accessory for your **CROCK-POT**® slow cooker. You can also use any straight-sided soufflé dish or deep cake pan that will fit into the stoneware of your unit. Baked goods can be prepared directly in the stoneware; however, they can be a little difficult to remove from the insert, so follow the recipe directions carefully.

SLOW COOKING 101

SIMMERING
❖ SOUPS ❖

Vegetable Soup with Beans

4 cups vegetable broth
1 can (about 15 ounces) cannellini beans, rinsed and drained
1 can (about 14 ounces) diced tomatoes
16 baby carrots
1 medium onion, chopped
1 ounce dried oyster mushrooms, chopped
3 tablespoons tomato paste

2 teaspoons garlic powder
1 teaspoon dried basil
1 teaspoon dried oregano
$1/2$ teaspoon dried rosemary
$1/2$ teaspoon dried marjoram
$1/2$ teaspoon dried sage
$1/2$ teaspoon dried thyme
$1/4$ teaspoon black pepper
French bread slices, toasted (optional)

Combine broth, beans, tomatoes, carrots, onion, mushrooms, tomato paste, garlic powder, basil, oregano, rosemary, marjoram, sage, thyme and pepper in **CROCK-POT**® slow cooker; stir to blend. Cover; cook on LOW 8 hours or on HIGH 4 hours. Serve with bread, if desired.

Makes 4 servings

Italian Wedding Soup with Three-Cheese Tortellini >

- 6 cups chicken broth
- 1 package (16 ounces) frozen Italian-style meatballs
- 2½ cups kale, stemmed and chopped
- 1 package (9 ounces) refrigerated three-cheese tortellini
- 1 cup celery, chopped
- 1 small onion, thinly sliced
- 1 teaspoon dried basil
  Juice of 1 lemon
- 1 tablespoon minced garlic
- ⅛ teaspoon salt
- ⅛ teaspoon sugar
  Black pepper

Combine broth, meatballs, kale, tortellini, celery, onion, basil, lemon juice, garlic, salt, sugar and pepper in **CROCK-POT®** slow cooker. Cover; cook on LOW 3 to 4 hours.

Makes 8 servings

Black Bean Soup

- 3 cans (15 ounces *each*) black beans, rinsed and drained
- 3½ cups beef broth
- 4 plum tomatoes, diced
- 2 jalapeño peppers, minced*
- ½ pound bacon, crisp-cooked and crumbled
- 1 large onion, chopped
- ⅓ cup red wine vinegar
- 1 teaspoon dried oregano
- 1½ teaspoons ground cumin
- 1 teaspoon dried thyme
  Salt and black pepper
  Optional toppings: diced avocado, lime juice and/or Cheddar cheese

*Jalapeño peppers can sting and irritate the skin, so wear rubber gloves when handling peppers and do not touch your eyes.

Combine beans, broth, tomatoes, jalapeño peppers, bacon, onion, vinegar, oregano, cumin, thyme, salt and black pepper in **CROCK-POT®** slow cooker; stir to blend. Cover; cook on LOW 8 to 10 hours or on HIGH 4 to 5 hours. Top each serving as desired.

Makes 4 to 6 servings

Country Sausage and Bean Soup >

2 cans (about **14** ounces *each*) chicken broth

1 can (about **15** ounces) black beans, rinsed and drained

1 cup chopped onion

1 cup chopped tomato

6 ounces country pork sausage, cooked and drained

1 tablespoon chili powder

1 tablespoon Worcestershire sauce

2 teaspoons extra virgin olive oil

2 whole bay leaves

1 1/2 teaspoons ground cumin

1 teaspoon sugar

1/2 teaspoon salt

1/8 teaspoon ground red pepper

1/4 cup chopped fresh cilantro (optional)

Combine broth, beans, onion, tomato, sausage, chili powder, Worcestershire sauce, oil, bay leaves, cumin, sugar, salt and ground red pepper in **CROCK-POT**® slow cooker. Cover; cook on LOW 4 hours or on HIGH 2 hours. Garnish with cilantro.

Makes 9 servings

Split Pea Soup with Ham

4 cups chicken broth

6 ounces ham, cut into 1/2-inch pieces

1 cup raw green split peas, rinsed and sorted

1 small onion, chopped

1 large carrot, chopped

2 stalks celery, trimmed and chopped

2 whole bay leaves

1 large clove garlic, minced

1/4 teaspoon dried thyme

1/8 teaspoon black pepper

Combine broth, ham, peas, onion, carrot, celery, bay leaves, garlic, thyme and pepper in **CROCK-POT**® slow cooker. Cover; cook on LOW 6 hours. Remove and discard bay leaves before serving.

Makes 4 servings

Simple Turkey Soup

2 pounds ground turkey, cooked and drained

1 can (about 28 ounces) whole tomatoes, undrained

2 cans (about 14 ounces *each*) beef broth

1 package (16 ounces) frozen mixed vegetables (such as carrots, beans, okra, corn or onion)

$1/2$ cup uncooked barley

1 teaspoon salt

1 teaspoon dried thyme

$1/2$ teaspoon ground coriander

Black pepper

Sprigs fresh thyme (optional)

Combine turkey, tomatoes, broth, vegetables, barley, salt, dried thyme, coriander and pepper in **CROCK-POT**® slow cooker; stir to blend. Add enough water to cover. Cover; cook on HIGH 3 to 4 hours. Garnish with thyme sprigs.

Makes 8 servings

Variations: Try adding other frozen or canned vegetables, diced potatoes and/or stewed tomatoes. For a large crowd, serve with cornbread.

Lentil Soup with Ham and Bacon

8 cups beef broth	³/₄ cup chopped tomatoes
3 cups dried lentils, rinsed and sorted	¹/₂ cup chopped onion
2 cups chopped ham	2 teaspoons salt
8 ounces chopped bacon, crisp-cooked and crumbled	2 teaspoons black pepper
1 cup chopped carrots	¹/₂ teaspoon dried marjoram
³/₄ cup chopped celery	Shredded mozzarella cheese (optional)
	Chopped fresh Italian parsley (optional)

Add broth, lentils, ham, bacon, carrots, celery, tomatoes, onion, salt, pepper and marjoram to **CROCK-POT®** slow cooker; stir to blend. Cover; cook on LOW 8 to 10 hours or on HIGH 6 to 8 hours. Garnish with cheese and parsley.

Makes 8 servings

✤ Tip

Make a simple soup into a super supper by serving it in individual bread bowls. Purchase small, round loaves of hearty bread, such as Italian or sourdough. Cut a small slice from the top and remove the inside of the loaf, leaving a 1¹/₂-inch shell. Pour in the soup and serve.

Chicken Soup >

6 cups chicken broth
1½ pounds boneless, skinless chicken breasts, cooked and cubed
2 cups sliced carrots
1 cup sliced mushrooms
1 red bell pepper, chopped
1 onion, chopped
2 tablespoons grated fresh ginger
3 teaspoons minced garlic
½ teaspoon red pepper flakes
Salt and black pepper

Combine broth, chicken, carrots, mushrooms, bell pepper, onion, ginger, garlic, red pepper flakes, salt and black pepper in **CROCK-POT®** slow cooker; stir to blend. Cover; cook on LOW 6 to 7 hours or on HIGH 3 to 3½ hours.

Makes 4 to 6 servings

Tex-Mex Split Pea Soup

6 cups water
1 package (16 ounces) dried split peas, rinsed and sorted
1 package (5 ounces) Canadian bacon, diced
3 medium carrots, thinly sliced
1 medium onion, chopped
3 chipotle peppers in adobo sauce, chopped plus 2 tablespoons adobo sauce reserved*
⅓ cup chopped fresh Italian parsley
1 tablespoon seasoned salt
2 cloves garlic, chopped
1 teaspoon black pepper
2 whole bay leaves
Optional toppings: croutons, sour cream and/or shredded cheese

Chipotle peppers can sting and irritate the skin, so wear rubber gloves when handling peppers and do not touch your eyes.

Combine water, peas, bacon, carrots, onion, chipotle peppers with 2 tablespoons sauce, parsley, seasoned salt, garlic, black pepper and bay leaves in **CROCK-POT®** slow cooker. Cover; cook on LOW 8 hours or on HIGH 4 hours. Remove and discard bay leaves. Top as desired.

Makes 8 servings

Linguiça and Green Bean Soup >

- 2 cans (about 15 ounces *each*) cut green beans, rinsed and drained
- 4 cups water
- 1 pound linguiça sausage links, cooked and cut into 1-inch pieces
- 1 can (about 15 ounces) kidney beans, rinsed and drained
- 1 large yellow onion, chopped
- 1 cup tomato juice
- 2 tablespoons olive oil
- 1 tablespoon Italian seasoning
- 3 cloves garlic, minced
- 2 teaspoons garlic salt
- 1 teaspoon ground cumin
- 1 whole bay leaf
- Prepared cornbread (optional)

Combine green beans, water, sausage, kidney beans, onion, tomato juice, oil, Italian seasoning, garlic, garlic salt, cumin and bay leaf in **CROCK-POT®** slow cooker. Cover; cook on LOW 8 to 10 hours or on HIGH 4 to 6 hours. Remove and discard bay leaf. Serve with cornbread, if desired.

Makes 6 servings

Spicy Thai Coconut Soup

- 3 cups coarsely shredded cooked chicken (about 12 ounces)
- 2 cups chicken broth
- 1 can (15 ounces) straw mushrooms, drained
- 1 can (13½ ounces) unsweetened coconut milk
- 1 can (about 8 ounces) baby corn, drained
- 1 tablespoon minced fresh ginger
- ½ to 1 teaspoon red curry paste
- 2 tablespoons lime juice (optional)
- ¼ cup chopped fresh cilantro (optional)

Combine chicken, broth, mushrooms, coconut milk, corn, ginger and curry paste in **CROCK-POT®** slow cooker. Cover; cook on HIGH 2 to 3 hours. Stir in lime juice, if desired. Sprinkle each serving with cilantro, if desired.

Makes 4 servings

Vegetable and Red Lentil Soup

1   can (about 14 ounces) vegetable broth

1   can (about 14 ounces) diced tomatoes

2   medium zucchini or yellow summer squash, chopped

1   red or yellow bell pepper, chopped

$^1/_2$ cup thinly sliced carrot

$^1/_2$ cup dried red lentils, rinsed and sorted

$^1/_2$ teaspoon salt

$^1/_2$ teaspoon sugar

$^1/_4$ teaspoon black pepper

2   tablespoons chopped fresh basil or thyme (optional)

$^1/_2$ cup croutons or shredded cheese (optional)

Combine broth, tomatoes, zucchini, bell pepper, carrot, lentils, salt, sugar and black pepper in **CROCK-POT**® slow cooker; stir to blend. Cover; cook on LOW 8 hours or on HIGH 4 hours. Garnish with basil and croutons.

Makes 6 servings

 Tip

If you would like to adapt your favorite soup recipe for a **CROCK-POT**® *slow cooker, reduce the liquid by as much as half, because foods don't lose as much moisture during slow cooking as during conventional cooking.*

Mexican Cheese Soup >

1 pound pasteurized process cheese product, cubed

1 pound ground beef, cooked and drained

1 can (about 15 ounces) kidney beans, rinsed and drained

1 can (about 14 ounces) diced tomatoes with mild green chiles, undrained

1 can (about 14 ounces) stewed tomatoes

1 can (8¾ ounces) corn

1 envelope taco seasoning

1 jalapeño pepper, seeded and diced (optional)*

Tortilla chips (optional)

Jalapeño peppers can sting and irritate the skin, so wear rubber gloves when handling peppers and do not touch your eyes.

Coat inside of **CROCK-POT®** slow cooker with nonstick cooking spray. Add cheese product, beef, beans, tomatoes with chiles, stewed tomatoes, corn, taco seasoning and jalapeño pepper, if desired; stir to blend. Cover; cook on LOW 4 to 5 hours or on HIGH 3 hours. Serve with tortilla chips, if desired.

Makes 6 to 8 servings

Mother's Sausage and Vegetable Soup

1 can (about 15 ounces) black beans, rinsed and drained

1 can (about 14 ounces) diced tomatoes

1 can (10¾ ounces) condensed cream of mushroom soup, undiluted

½ pound smoked turkey sausage, cut into ½-inch slices

2 cups diced potatoes

1 cup chopped onion

1 cup chopped red bell pepper

½ cup water

2 teaspoons prepared horseradish

2 teaspoons honey

1 teaspoon dried basil

Combine beans, tomatoes, soup, turkey sausage, potatoes, onion, pepper, water, horseradish, honey and basil in **CROCK-POT®** slow cooker; stir to blend. Cover; cook on LOW 7 to 8 hours.

Makes 6 to 8 servings

Turkey-Tomato Soup >

2 medium boneless turkey thighs, cut into 1-inch pieces
1¾ cups chicken broth
1½ cups frozen corn
2 small white or red potatoes, cubed
1 cup chopped onion
1 cup water
1 can (about 8 ounces) tomato sauce

¼ cup tomato paste
2 tablespoons Dijon mustard
1 teaspoon hot pepper sauce
½ teaspoon sugar
½ teaspoon garlic powder
¼ cup finely chopped fresh Italian parsley (optional)

Combine turkey, broth, corn, potatoes, onion, water, tomato sauce, tomato paste, mustard, hot pepper sauce, sugar and garlic powder in **CROCK-POT®** slow cooker. Cover; cook on LOW 9 to 10 hours. Garnish each serving with parsley.

Makes 6 servings

Hearty Mushroom and Barley Soup

9 cups chicken broth
1 package (16 ounces) sliced mushrooms
1 onion, chopped
2 carrots, chopped
2 stalks celery, chopped

½ cup uncooked pearl barley
½ ounce dried porcini mushrooms
3 cloves garlic, minced
1 teaspoon salt
½ teaspoon dried thyme
½ teaspoon black pepper

Combine broth, sliced mushrooms, onion, carrots, celery, barley, dried mushrooms, garlic, salt, thyme and pepper in **CROCK-POT®** slow cooker; stir to blend. Cover; cook on LOW 4 to 6 hours.

Makes 8 to 10 servings

Chicken Fiesta Soup >

4 boneless, skinless chicken breasts, cooked and shredded
1 can (28 ounces) enchilada sauce
1 can (about 14 ounces) chicken broth
1 can (about 14 ounces) stewed tomatoes, drained
1 yellow squash, diced
1 zucchini, diced
1 cup frozen corn
1 cup finely chopped onion

2 cans (4 ounces *each*) chopped mild green chiles
¼ cup finely chopped fresh cilantro
2 cloves garlic, minced
1 teaspoon ground cumin
1 teaspoon chili powder
1 teaspoon salt
¾ teaspoon black pepper
8 tostada shells, crumbled (optional)
2 cups (8 ounces) shredded Cheddar cheese (optional)

Combine chicken, enchilada sauce, broth, tomatoes, squash, zucchini, corn, onion, chiles, cilantro, garlic, cumin, chili powder, salt and black pepper in **CROCK-POT®** slow cooker. Cover; cook on LOW 8 hours. Top each serving with crumbled tostada shells and cheese, if desired.

Makes 8 servings

Beef Fajita Soup

1 pound cubed beef stew meat
1 can (about 15 ounces) pinto beans, rinsed and drained
1 can (about 15 ounces) black beans, rinsed and drained
1 can (about 14 ounces) diced tomatoes with roasted garlic
1 can (about 14 ounces) beef broth

1½ cups water
1 green bell pepper, thinly sliced
1 red bell pepper, thinly sliced
1 onion, thinly sliced
2 teaspoons ground cumin
1 teaspoon seasoned salt
1 teaspoon black pepper

Combine beef, beans, tomatoes, broth, water, bell peppers, onion, cumin, salt and black pepper in **CROCK-POT®** slow cooker; stir to blend. Cover; cook on LOW 8 hours.

Makes 8 servings

Hearty Lentil and Barley Soup

5 to 6 cups water

1 can (about 14 ounces) diced tomatoes with green pepper, celery and onion

8 ounces smoked sausage, cut into $1/2$-inch slices

$3/4$ cup dried brown or red lentils, rinsed and sorted

$1/2$ cup uncooked medium pearl barley

$1/4$ cup sun-dried tomato halves, cut into pieces

2 tablespoons dried vegetable flakes

1 tablespoon fresh oregano *or* 1 teaspoon dried oregano

1 tablespoon minced onion

2 teaspoons chicken bouillon granules

$1/2$ teaspoon black pepper

$1/2$ teaspoon minced garlic

$1/8$ teaspoon red pepper flakes (optional)

Lemon-pepper seasoning (optional)

Combine water, diced tomatoes, sausage, lentils, barley, sun-dried tomatoes, vegetable flakes, oregano, onion, bouillon granules, black pepper, garlic and red pepper flakes, if desired, in **CROCK-POT**® slow cooker; stir to blend. Cover; cook on LOW 6 to 8 hours. Season with lemon-pepper before serving, if desired.

Makes 10 to 12 servings

❖ Tip

Lentils come in brown (the most common), red and yellow. All varieties can be used interchangeably in cooking, but the red variety cooks more quickly.

Navy Bean and Ham Soup >

6 cups water

5 cups dried navy beans, soaked overnight, rinsed and drained

1 pound ham, cubed

1 can (about 15 ounces) corn, drained

1 can (about 4 ounces) diced mild green chiles, drained

1 onion, diced

Salt and black pepper

Combine water, beans, ham, corn, chiles, onion, salt and pepper in **CROCK-POT®** slow cooker. Cover; cook on LOW 8 to 10 hours

Makes 6 servings

Veggie Soup with Beef

2 cans (15 ounces *each*) mixed vegetables

1 pound cubed beef stew meat

1 can (8 ounces) tomato sauce

2 cloves garlic, minced

Combine vegetables, beef, tomato sauce and garlic in **CROCK-POT®** slow cooker; stir to blend. Add enough water to fill **CROCK-POT®** slow cooker to within 1/2 inch of top. Cover; cook on LOW 8 to 10 hours.

Makes 4 servings

Rustic Vegetable Soup >

1 jar (16 ounces) picante sauce
1 package (10 ounces) frozen mixed vegetables
1 package (10 ounces) frozen cut green beans
1 can (about 10 ounces) condensed beef broth, undiluted
1 to 2 baking potatoes, cut into $1/2$-inch pieces
1 medium green bell pepper, chopped
$1/2$ teaspoon sugar
$1/4$ cup finely chopped fresh Italian parsley (optional)

Combine picante sauce, mixed vegetables, green beans, broth, potatoes, bell pepper and sugar in **CROCK-POT®** slow cooker; stir to blend. Cover; cook on LOW 8 hours or on HIGH 4 hours. Garnish with parsley.

Makes 8 servings

Fiesta Black Bean Soup

6 cups chicken broth
$3/4$ cup diced potatoes
1 can (about 15 ounces) black beans, rinsed and drained
$1/2$ pound cooked ham, chopped
$1/2$ onion, chopped
1 can (4 ounces) diced mild green chiles
2 cloves garlic, minced
2 teaspoons dried oregano
$1 1/2$ teaspoons dried thyme
1 teaspoon ground cumin
Optional toppings: sour cream, chopped bell peppers and chopped tomatoes

Combine broth, potatoes, beans, ham, onion, chiles, garlic, oregano, thyme and cumin in **CROCK-POT®** slow cooker; stir to blend. Cover; cook on LOW 8 to 10 hours or on HIGH 4 to 5 hours. Top each serving as desired.

Makes 6 to 8 servings

Lentil and Portobello Soup >

1 can (28 ounces) diced tomatoes

1 can (about 14 ounces) vegetable broth

2 portobello mushrooms (about 8 ounces total), cut into $\frac{1}{2}$-inch pieces

1 medium onion, chopped

2 medium carrots, cut into $\frac{1}{2}$-inch-thick rounds

1 cup dried lentils, rinsed and sorted

1 tablespoon olive oil

2 cloves garlic, minced

1 teaspoon dried rosemary

1 whole bay leaf

Salt and black pepper

Combine tomatoes, broth, mushrooms, onion, carrots, lentils, oil, garlic, rosemary and bay leaf, salt and pepper in **CROCK-POT®** slow cooker; stir to blend. Cover; cook on HIGH 5 to 6 hours. Remove and discard bay leaf before serving.

Makes 6 servings

Chicken and Wild Rice Soup

3 cans (about 14 ounces *each*) chicken broth

1 pound boneless, skinless chicken breasts or thighs, cut into 1-inch pieces

2 cups water

1 cup sliced celery

1 cup diced carrots

1 package (6 ounces) converted long grain and wild rice mix with seasoning packet (not quick-cooking or instant rice)

$\frac{1}{2}$ cup chopped onion

$\frac{1}{2}$ teaspoon black pepper

2 teaspoons white vinegar (optional)

Chopped fresh Italian parsley (optional)

Combine broth, chicken, water, celery, carrots, rice and seasoning packet, onion and pepper in **CROCK-POT®** slow cooker; stir to blend. Cover; cook on LOW 6 to 7 hours or on HIGH 4 to 5 hours. Stir in vinegar, if desired. Garnish each serving with parsley.

Makes 9 servings

Hamburger Veggie Soup >

1 pound ground beef, cooked and drained

1 bag (16 ounces) frozen mixed vegetables

1 package (10 ounces) frozen seasoning blend vegetables

1 can (about 14 ounces) stewed tomatoes, undrained

1 can (10¾ ounces) condensed tomato soup, undiluted

2 cans (5½ ounces *each*) spicy vegetable juice

Salt and black pepper

Coat inside of **CROCK-POT**® slow cooker with nonstick cooking spray. Combine beef, frozen vegetables, tomatoes, soup, juice, salt and pepper in **CROCK-POT**® slow cooker; stir to blend. Cover; cook on HIGH 4 hours.

Makes 4 to 6 servings

Winter's Best Bean Soup

10 cups chicken broth

3 cans (about 15 ounces *each*) cannellini beans, rinsed and drained

1 can (about 14 ounces) diced tomatoes

1 package (10 ounces) frozen sliced or diced carrots

1 onion, chopped

6 ounces bacon, crisp-cooked and crumbled

2 teaspoons minced garlic

1 sprig fresh rosemary

1 teaspoon black pepper

Combine broth, beans, tomatoes, carrots, onion, bacon, garlic, rosemary and pepper in **CROCK-POT**® slow cooker; stir to blend. Cover; cook on LOW 8 hours. Remove rosemary sprig before serving.

Makes 8 to 10 servings

Serving Suggestion: Place slices of toasted Italian bread in bottom of individual soup bowls. Drizzle with olive oil. Pour soup over bread and serve.

CHICKEN
✦ FAVORITES ✦

Moroccan Chicken Stew

1 pound boneless, skinless chicken thighs, cut into 2-inch pieces	**2 tablespoons olive oil**
¹⁄₂ cup chopped celery	**3 cloves garlic, minced**
¹⁄₂ cup chopped carrots	**3 whole bay leaves**
2 ounces chopped prunes	**¹⁄₂ teaspoon ground cinnamon**
¹⁄₂ to ³⁄₄ cup dry white wine	**¹⁄₂ teaspoon ground coriander**
¹⁄₃ cup white balsamic vinegar	**¹⁄₄ teaspoon dried oregano**
¹⁄₄ cup packed brown sugar	**Pinch black pepper**
	Pinch ground ginger

Combine chicken, celery, carrots, prunes, wine, vinegar, brown sugar, oil, garlic, bay leaves, cinnamon, coriander, oregano, pepper and ginger in **CROCK-POT®** slow cooker. Cover; cook on LOW 3 to 4 hours. Remove and discard bay leaves before serving.

Makes 4 servings

East Indian Curried Chicken with Capers >

1½ pounds boneless, skinless chicken breasts
2 cups ripe plum tomatoes, diced
1 cup artichoke hearts, drained and chopped
1 cup chicken broth
1 medium red onion, chopped
⅓ cup dry white wine

¼ cup capers, drained
2 tablespoons quick-cooking tapioca
2 teaspoons curry powder
½ teaspoon ground thyme
¼ teaspoon salt
¼ teaspoon black pepper
4 cups cooked brown rice (optional)

Combine chicken, tomatoes, artichokes, broth, onion, wine, capers, tapioca, curry powder, thyme, salt and pepper in **CROCK-POT®** slow cooker; stir to blend. Cover; cook on LOW 7 to 9 hours or on HIGH 3 to 4 hours. Serve chicken and vegetables over rice, if desired. Spoon sauce over chicken.

Makes 6 servings

Favorite Chicken

1 whole chicken (about 3 pounds), cut into pieces
1 cup chopped onion
1 cup sliced celery
1 cup sliced carrots
½ teaspoon seasoned salt
½ teaspoon black pepper

¼ teaspoon garlic powder
¼ teaspoon poultry seasoning
3 to 4 medium potatoes, cut into slices
1 can (about 14 ounces) chicken broth

Place chicken, onion, celery, carrots, seasoned salt, pepper, garlic powder and poultry seasoning in **CROCK-POT®** slow cooker. Top with potatoes. Add broth. Cover; cook on LOW 6 to 8 hours.

Makes 4 servings

Angel Wings

10 chicken wings
1 can (10¾ ounces) condensed tomato soup, undiluted
¾ cup water

¼ cup packed light brown sugar
2½ tablespoons balsamic vinegar
2 tablespoons chopped shallots

Combine chicken, soup, water, brown sugar, vinegar and shallots in **CROCK-POT**® slow cooker; stir to blend. Cover; cook on LOW 5 to 6 hours.

Makes 5 servings

✤ Tip

*To reheat leftover foods, don't use the **CROCK-POT**® slow cooker. Remove cooled leftovers to a resealable food storage bag or storage container with a tight-fitting lid and refrigerate. Use a microwave oven, the stove top or an oven for reheating.*

Chicken Provençal

- **2 pounds boneless, skinless chicken thighs, cut into quarters**
- **2 medium red bell peppers, cut into $^1/_4$-inch-thick slices**
- **1 medium yellow bell pepper, cut into $^1/_4$-inch-thick slices**
- **1 onion, thinly sliced**
- **1 can (28 ounces) plum tomatoes, drained**
- **3 cloves garlic, minced**
- **$^1/_4$ teaspoon salt**
- **$^1/_4$ teaspoon dried thyme**
- **$^1/_4$ teaspoon ground fennel seed**
- **3 strips orange peel**
- **$^1/_2$ cup fresh basil leaves, chopped (optional)**

Combine chicken, bell peppers, onion, tomatoes, garlic, salt, thyme, fennel seed and orange peel in **CROCK-POT**® slow cooker; stir to blend. Cover; cook on LOW 7 to 9 hours or on HIGH 3 to 4 hours. Garnish each serving with basil.

Makes 8 servings

Note: Recipe can be doubled for a 5-, 6- or 7-quart **CROCK-POT**® slow cooker.

Slow Cooker Chicken and Dressing >

4 boneless, skinless chicken breasts (about 1 pound)
   Salt and black pepper
4 slices Swiss cheese
2 cans (10¾ ounces *each*) condensed cream of chicken, celery or mushroom soup, undiluted

1 can (about 14 ounces) chicken broth
3 cups packaged stuffing mix
½ cup (1 stick) butter, melted

Place chicken in **CROCK-POT**® slow cooker. Season with salt and pepper. Top each breast with cheese slice. Add soup and broth; sprinkle stuffing mix over top. Pour melted butter over all ingredients in **CROCK-POT**® slow cooker. Cover; cook on LOW 6 to 8 hours or on HIGH 3 to 4 hours.

Makes 4 servings

3-Cheese Chicken and Noodles

3 cups chopped cooked chicken
1½ cups cottage cheese
1 can (10¾ ounces) condensed cream of chicken soup, undiluted
1 package (8 ounces) wide egg noodles, cooked and drained
1 cup (4 ounces) shredded Monterey Jack cheese
½ cup grated Parmesan cheese
½ cup diced onion

½ cup diced celery
½ cup diced green bell pepper
½ cup diced red bell pepper
½ cup chicken broth
1 can (4 ounces) sliced mushrooms, drained
2 tablespoons butter, melted
½ teaspoon dried thyme
   Crusty rolls and asparagus (optional)

Combine chicken, cottage cheese, soup, noodles, cheeses, onion, celery, bell peppers, broth, mushrooms, butter and thyme in **CROCK-POT**® slow cooker; stir to blend. Cover; cook on LOW 6 to 8 hours or on HIGH 3 to 4 hours. Serve with rolls and asparagus, if desired.

Makes 6 servings

Japanese-Style Simmered Chicken Thighs

2 pounds boneless, skinless chicken thighs

1/2 pound shiitake mushrooms, stemmed and quartered

3 medium carrots, cut into 2-inch pieces

1 medium Japanese eggplant, halved lengthwise and cut into 1/2-inch-thick slices

1 medium onion, cut into 1-inch pieces

1/2 cup sugar

1/2 cup soy sauce

1/3 cup chicken broth

1/4 cup mirin

1 tablespoon cornstarch

1 teaspoon grated fresh ginger

1 teaspoon minced garlic

1 star anise pod*
   Hot cooked rice (optional)

1 tablespoon sesame seeds, toasted** (optional)

Or substitute 1/4 teaspoon Chinese five-spice powder.

**To toast sesame seeds, spread in small, dry skillet. Shake skillet over medium-low heat 2 minutes or until seeds begin to pop and turn golden brown.*

Combine chicken, mushrooms, carrots, eggplant, onion, sugar, soy sauce, broth, mirin, cornstarch, ginger, garlic and star anise in **CROCK-POT**® slow cooker; stir to blend. Cover; cook on LOW 7 hours. Remove and discard star anise. Serve chicken, vegetables and sauce over rice, if desired. Garnish with sesame seeds.

Makes 4 servings

Chicken and Sweet Potato Stew

4 boneless, skinless chicken breasts, cut into 1-inch pieces

2 medium sweet potatoes, cubed

2 medium Yukon Gold potatoes, cubed

2 medium carrots, cut into $1/2$-inch slices

1 can (28 ounces) whole stewed tomatoes

1 cup chicken broth

1 teaspoon salt

1 teaspoon paprika

1 teaspoon celery seeds

$1/2$ teaspoon black pepper

$1/8$ teaspoon ground cinnamon

$1/8$ teaspoon ground nutmeg

$1/4$ cup chopped fresh basil (optional)

Combine chicken, sweet potatoes, Yukon Gold potatoes, carrots, tomatoes, broth, salt, paprika, celery seeds, pepper, cinnamon and nutmeg in **CROCK-POT®** slow cooker. Cover; cook on LOW 6 to 8 hours or on HIGH 3 to 4 hours. Garnish each serving with basil.

Makes 6 servings

✤ Tip

After purchasing sweet potatoes, brush off any dirt but do not wash them. Sweet potatoes should be handled gently since their skins are very thin. Store them in a cool, dry and dark location. They will keep up to a month at about 55°F. Do not refrigerate sweet potatoes, because they can develop an off flavor.

Herbed Chicken and Vegetable Barley Pilaf >

8 small bone-in chicken thighs (about 2¼ pounds)
1½ cups chicken broth
1 cup sliced carrots
¾ cup uncooked pearl barley
½ cup chopped onion

1 teaspoon garlic salt
1 teaspoon paprika
½ teaspoon dried thyme
½ teaspoon dried rosemary
Chopped fresh Italian parsley (optional)

Combine chicken, broth, carrots, barley, onion, garlic salt, paprika, thyme and rosemary in **CROCK-POT®** slow cooker. Cover; cook on LOW 5 to 6 hours or on HIGH 2½ to 3 hours. Garnish each serving with parsley.

Makes 4 servings

Tender Asian-Style Chicken

6 to 8 boneless, skinless chicken thighs, coated with all-purpose flour, salt and black pepper
¼ cup soy sauce
2 tablespoons rice wine vinegar
2 tablespoons ketchup
1 tablespoon packed brown sugar

1 clove garlic, minced
½ teaspoon grated fresh ginger *or* ¼ teaspoon ground ginger
¼ teaspoon red pepper flakes
Hot cooked rice (optional)
Chopped fresh cilantro (optional)

Combine chicken, soy sauce, vinegar, ketchup, brown sugar, garlic, ginger and red pepper flakes in **CROCK-POT®** slow cooker. Cover; cook on LOW 5 to 6 hours. Serve with rice, if desired. Garnish with cilantro.

Makes 4 to 6 servings

Tropical Chicken Wings >

3 pounds chicken wings, tips removed and split at joints

1 jar (12 ounces) pineapple preserves

1/2 cup chopped green onions

1/2 cup soy sauce

3 tablespoons lime juice

2 tablespoons honey

1 tablespoon minced garlic

2 teaspoons spicy chili sauce

1/4 teaspoon ground allspice

1 tablespoon toasted sesame seeds* (optional)

To toast sesame seeds, spread in small skillet. Shake skillet over medium heat 2 minutes or until seeds begin to pop and turn golden brown.

Combine wings, preserves, green onions, soy sauce, lime juice, honey, garlic, chili sauce and allspice in **CROCK-POT**® slow cooker; stir to blend. Cover; cook on LOW 3 to 4 hours. Sprinkle with sesame seeds, if desired.

Makes 6 to 8 servings

Chicken, Fennel and White Beans

3 bulbs fennel, thinly sliced (about 6 cups)

1 can (about 15 ounces) cannellini beans, rinsed and drained

1/2 cup dry white wine

1 shallot, finely chopped

1 clove garlic, minced

6 skinless chicken thighs

6 skinless chicken legs

1 teaspoon salt

1/2 teaspoon dried rosemary

1/4 teaspoon black pepper

1 lemon, thinly sliced

1/4 cup grated Parmesan cheese (optional)

Combine fennel, beans, wine, shallot and garlic in **CROCK-POT**® slow cooker. Top with chicken, salt, rosemary and pepper. Place lemon slices over chicken. Cover; cook on LOW 4 to 6 hours or on HIGH 2 to 3 hours. Serve with cooking liquid. Garnish with cheese.

Makes 6 servings

Pollo Ranchero (Country Chicken) >

1 whole chicken (2 to 3 pounds),
  cut into pieces
5 cups chopped tomatoes
2 cups water
1 cup chopped ham
1 large onion, chopped
2 jalapeño peppers, minced*
4 sprigs fresh tarragon

2 tablespoons seasoned salt
2 tablespoons onion powder
2 tablespoons garlic powder
2 tablespoons tomato paste
  Hot cooked rice (optional)

Jalapeño peppers can sting and irritate the skin, so wear rubber gloves when handling peppers and do not touch your eyes.

Combine chicken, tomatoes, water, ham, onion, jalapeño peppers, tarragon, seasoned salt, onion powder, garlic powder and tomato paste in **CROCK-POT®** slow cooker. Cover; cook on HIGH 3 to 4 hours. Serve over rice, if desired.

Makes 4 servings

Thai Chicken

2½ pounds chicken pieces
1 cup salsa
¼ cup peanut butter
2 tablespoons lime juice
1 tablespoon soy sauce

1 teaspoon minced fresh ginger
  Hot cooked rice (optional)
½ cup peanuts, chopped (optional)
2 tablespoons chopped fresh
  cilantro (optional)

Combine chicken, salsa, peanut butter, lime juice, soy sauce and ginger in **CROCK-POT®** slow cooker. Cover; cook on LOW 8 to 9 hours or on HIGH 3 to 4 hours. Serve over rice, if desired. Garnish with peanuts and cilantro.

Makes 6 servings

Hearty Chicken Chili

2 cans (about **15 ounces** *each*)
hominy, rinsed and drained*

1½ pounds boneless, skinless chicken
thighs, cut into 1-inch pieces

1 can (about **15 ounces**) pinto beans,
rinsed and drained

1 medium onion, finely chopped

1 cup chicken broth

1 small jalapeño pepper, seeded and
minced**

1 clove garlic, minced

1½ teaspoons chili powder

¾ teaspoon salt

½ teaspoon ground cumin

½ teaspoon dried oregano

½ teaspoon black pepper
Chopped fresh Italian parsley
or cilantro (optional)

*Hominy is corn that has been treated to remove
the germ and hull. It can be found with the canned
vegetables or beans in most supermarkets.*

**Jalapeño peppers can sting and irritate the skin, so
wear rubber gloves when handling peppers and do not
touch your eyes.*

Combine hominy, chicken, beans, onion, broth, jalapeño pepper, garlic, chili powder, salt, cumin, oregano and black pepper in **CROCK-POT®** slow cooker. Cover; cook on LOW 7 hours. Garnish with parsley.

Makes 6 servings

Variations: For a hotter dish, add ¼ teaspoon red pepper flakes with the seasonings. For a thicker chili, stir 3 tablespoons cooking liquid into 1 tablespoon flour in small bowl until smooth. Whisk into cooking liquid. Cover; cook on HIGH 10 minutes or until thickened.

Herbed Artichoke Chicken

1½ pounds boneless, skinless chicken breasts
1 can (14 ounces) artichoke hearts in water, drained
1 can (about 14 ounces) diced tomatoes, drained
1 small onion, chopped
1 cup chicken broth
½ cup kalamata olives, pitted and sliced
¼ cup dry white wine
3 tablespoons quick-cooking tapioca
1 tablespoon chopped fresh Italian parsley
2 teaspoons curry powder
1 teaspoon dried sweet basil
1 teaspoon dried thyme
½ teaspoon salt
½ teaspoon black pepper

Combine chicken, artichokes, tomatoes, onion, broth, olives, wine, tapioca, parsley, curry powder, basil, thyme, salt and pepper in **CROCK-POT®** slow cooker; stir to blend. Cover; cook on LOW 6 to 8 hours or on HIGH 3½ to 4 hours.

Makes 6 servings

❖ Tip

*For a 5-, 6- or 7-quart **CROCK-POT®** slow cooker, double all ingredients, except for the chicken broth and dry white wine. Increase the broth and wine amounts by only one and a half.*

Mediterranean Chicken

- **2 pounds boneless, skinless chicken breasts**
- **1 can (28 ounces) diced tomatoes**
- **2 onions, chopped**
- **1/2 cup dry sherry**
- **6 teaspoons minced garlic**

- **Juice of 2 lemons**
- **2 cinnamon sticks**
- **1 whole bay leaf**
- **1/2 teaspoon black pepper**
- **Hot cooked egg noodles (optional)**
- **1/2 cup feta cheese (optional)**

Combine chicken, tomatoes, onions, sherry, garlic, lemon juice, cinnamon sticks, bay leaf and pepper in **CROCK-POT**® slow cooker. Cover; cook on LOW 8 to 10 hours or on HIGH 4 to 5 hours. Remove and discard cinnamon sticks and bay leaf. Serve chicken and sauce over noodles, if desired. Garnish with cheese.

Makes 6 servings

Cashew Chicken >

6 boneless, skinless chicken breasts
1½ cups cashew nuts
1 cup sliced mushrooms
1 cup sliced celery
1 can (10¾ ounces) condensed
   cream of mushroom soup,
   undiluted

¼ cup chopped green onions
2 tablespoons butter
1½ tablespoons soy sauce
   Hot cooked rice (optional)

Combine chicken, cashews, mushrooms, celery, soup, green onions, butter and soy sauce in **CROCK-POT®** slow cooker. Cover; cook on LOW 6 to 8 hours or on HIGH 4 to 6 hours. Serve over rice, if desired.

Makes 6 servings

Cheesy Slow Cooker Chicken

6 boneless, skinless chicken breasts
2 cans (10½ ounces *each*)
   condensed cream of chicken
   soup, undiluted
1 can (10½ ounces) condensed
   Cheddar cheese soup, undiluted

1 teaspoon garlic powder
   Salt and black pepper
   Hot cooked pasta, rice or mashed
   potatoes (optional)
   Chopped fresh Italian parsley
   (optional)

Combine chicken, soups, garlic powder, salt and pepper in **CROCK-POT®** slow cooker. Cover; cook on LOW 6 to 8 hours. Serve over pasta, if desired. Garnish with parsley.

Makes 6 servings

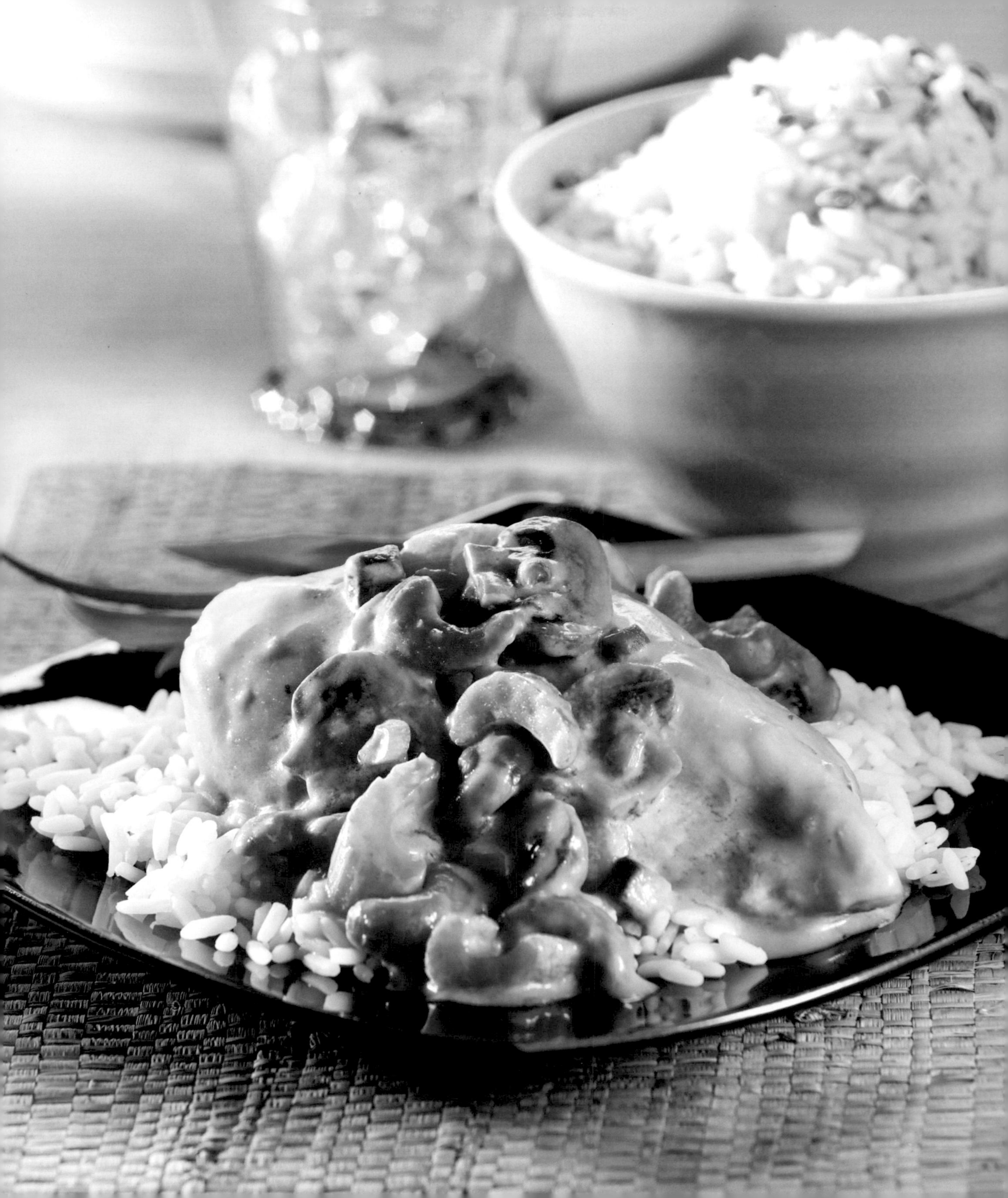

Chipotle Chicken Casserole

1 pound boneless, skinless chicken thighs, cut into 1-inch pieces

1½ cups chicken broth

1 can (about 15 ounces) navy beans, rinsed and drained

1 can (about 15 ounces) black beans, rinsed and drained

1 can (about 14 ounces) crushed tomatoes, undrained

½ cup orange juice

1 medium onion, diced

1 canned chipotle pepper in adobo sauce, minced

1 teaspoon salt

1 teaspoon ground cumin

1 whole bay leaf

¼ cup chopped fresh cilantro (optional)

Combine chicken, broth, beans, tomatoes, orange juice, onion, chipotle pepper, salt, cumin and bay leaf in **CROCK-POT®** slow cooker. Cover; cook on LOW 7 to 8 hours or on HIGH 3½ to 4 hours. Remove and discard bay leaf. Garnish with cilantro.

Makes 6 servings

Chicken with Mushrooms >

8 boneless, skinless chicken breasts
  (2 pounds total), cut into pieces
3 cups sliced mushrooms
1 large onion, chopped
1 can (6 ounces) tomato paste
½ cup chicken broth
¼ cup dry red wine
2 tablespoons quick-cooking tapioca

2 cloves garlic, minced
2 teaspoons sugar
2 teaspoons dried basil
  Salt and black pepper
  Hot cooked noodles or rice
  (optional)
  Grated Parmesan cheese
  (optional)

Combine chicken, mushrooms, onion, tomato paste, broth, wine, tapioca, garlic, sugar, basil, salt and pepper in **CROCK-POT®** slow cooker. Cover; cook on LOW 7 to 8 hours or on HIGH 3 to 4 hours. Serve over noodles, if desired. Garnish with cheese.

Makes 4 servings

Chicken in Enchilada Sauce

1½ pounds boneless, skinless chicken
  thighs, cut into 1-inch pieces
1 can (about 14 ounces) diced
  tomatoes with mild green chiles*
1 can (10 ounces) enchilada sauce
1 cup frozen corn
2 tablespoons minced fresh cilantro

¼ teaspoon ground cumin
¼ teaspoon black pepper
½ cup (2 ounces) shredded
  mozzarella cheese (optional)
  Sliced green onions (optional)

You may substitute regular diced tomatoes plus ¼ teaspoon red pepper flakes.

Combine chicken, tomatoes, enchilada sauce, corn, cilantro, cumin and pepper in **CROCK-POT®** slow cooker. Cover; cook on LOW 6 to 7 hours. Top with cheese, if desired. Garnish with green onions.

Makes 4 servings

Chicken Pilaf >

2 pounds chopped cooked chicken
2½ cups water
2 cans (8 ounces *each*) tomato sauce
1⅓ cups uncooked long grain
    converted rice
1 cup chopped onion
1 cup chopped celery
1 cup chopped green bell pepper
⅔ cup sliced pitted black olives
¼ cup sliced almonds
¼ cup (½ stick) butter
2 cloves garlic, minced
2½ teaspoons salt
½ teaspoon ground allspice
½ teaspoon ground turmeric
¼ teaspoon curry powder
¼ teaspoon black pepper

Combine chicken, water, tomato sauce, rice, onion, celery, bell pepper, olives, almonds, butter, garlic, salt, allspice, turmeric, curry powder and black pepper in **CROCK-POT®** slow cooker; stir to blend. Cover; cook on LOW 6 to 8 hours or on HIGH 3 to 4 hours.

Makes 10 servings

Nice 'n' Easy Italian Chicken

4 boneless, skinless chicken breasts
    (about 1 pound)
1 jar (26 ounces) pasta sauce
1 medium green bell pepper,
    chopped
1 medium zucchini, diced
1 medium onion, chopped
8 ounces mushrooms, sliced
    Hot cooked linguini or spaghetti
    (optional)

Combine chicken, pasta sauce, bell pepper, zucchini, onion and mushrooms in **CROCK-POT®** slow cooker. Cover; cook on LOW 6 to 8 hours. Serve over linguini, if desired.

Makes 4 servings

Chicken and Butternut Squash >

6 boneless, skinless chicken thighs
  (1½ pounds total)
1 (1½- to 2-pound) butternut
  squash, cubed

2 tablespoons balsamic vinegar
4 cloves garlic, minced
6 fresh sage leaves
  Salt and black pepper

Combine chicken, squash, vinegar, garlic, sage, salt and pepper in **CROCK-POT®** slow cooker. Cover; cook on LOW 4 to 6 hours.

Makes 6 servings

Teriyaki Chicken Wings

3 to 4 pounds chicken wings
¼ cup soy sauce
¼ cup dry sherry
¼ cup honey
1 tablespoon hoisin sauce
1 tablespoon orange juice

2 cloves garlic, minced
1 fresh red chile pepper, finely
  chopped (optional)*

*Chile peppers can sting and irritate the skin, so wear rubber gloves when handling and do not touch your eyes.

Combine wings, soy sauce, sherry, honey, hoisin sauce, orange juice, garlic and chile pepper, if desired, in **CROCK-POT®** slow cooker. Cover; cook on LOW 3 to 3½ hours or on HIGH 1½ to 2 hours.

Makes 6 to 8 servings

Sweet Chicken Curry >

1	pound boneless, skinless chicken breasts, cut into 1-inch pieces	1/2	cup prepared mango chutney
1	large green or red bell pepper, cut into 1-inch pieces	1/4	cup water
		2	tablespoons cornstarch
1	large onion, sliced	1 1/2	teaspoons curry powder
1	large tomato, chopped		Hot cooked rice (optional)

Combine chicken, bell pepper, onion, tomato, chutney, water, cornstarch and curry powder in **CROCK-POT®** slow cooker; stir to blend. Cover; cook on LOW 3 1/2 to 4 1/2 hours. Serve over rice, if desired.

Makes 4 servings

Hot and Sour Chicken

4	to 6 boneless, skinless chicken breasts (1 to 1 1/2 pounds total)	1	package (about 1 ounce) dry hot-and-sour soup mix
1	cup chicken or vegetable broth		

Combine chicken, broth and soup mix in **CROCK-POT®** slow cooker. Cover; cook on LOW 5 to 6 hours.

Makes 4 to 6 servings

Serving Suggestion: Serve this dish over a bed of sugar snap peas tossed with diced red bell pepper.

Savory Chicken and Oregano Chili >

3 cans (about 15 ounces *each*) cannellini beans, rinsed and drained

3¹⁄₂ cups chicken broth

2 cups chopped cooked chicken

2 red bell peppers, chopped

1 onion, chopped

1 can (4 ounces) diced mild green chiles, drained

3 cloves garlic, minced

2 teaspoons ground cumin

1 teaspoon salt

1 tablespoon minced fresh oregano (optional)

Combine beans, broth, chicken, bell peppers, onion, chiles, garlic, cumin and salt in **CROCK-POT**® slow cooker; stir to blend. Cover; cook on LOW 8 to 10 hours or on HIGH 4 to 5 hours. Garnish each serving with oregano.

Makes 8 servings

Moroccan Spiced Chicken Wings

5 pounds chicken wings, tips removed and split at joints

¹⁄₄ cup orange juice

3 tablespoons tomato paste

2 teaspoons ground cumin

1 teaspoon salt

1 teaspoon curry powder

1 teaspoon ground ginger

1 teaspoon ground cinnamon

Combine wings, orange juice, tomato paste, cumin, salt, curry powder, ginger and cinnamon in **CROCK-POT**® slow cooker; stir to blend. Cover; cook on LOW 6 to 7 hours or on HIGH 3 to 4 hours.

Makes 8 servings

BEEF
✦ DINNERS ✦

Horseradish Roast Beef and Potatoes

3 **pounds beef roast***

1 **tablespoon minced fresh Italian parsley**

1 **teaspoon dried thyme**

1 **tablespoon freshly grated horseradish**

1 **tablespoon Dijon mustard**

1 **to 2 pounds Yukon Gold potatoes, quartered**

1 **pound mushrooms, cut into large pieces**

2 **cans (about 14 ounces *each*) beef broth**

2 **large tomatoes, diced**

1 **large onion, sliced**

1 **green bell pepper, chopped**

1 **red bell pepper, chopped**

1 **cup dry red wine**

3 **cloves garlic, minced**

1 **whole bay leaf**

 Salt and black pepper

*Unless you have a 5-, 6- or 7-quart CROCK-POT® slow cooker, cut any roast larger than 2$\frac{1}{2}$ pounds in half so it cooks completely.

Combine roast, parsley, thyme, horseradish and mustard in **CROCK-POT®** slow cooker. Add potatoes, mushrooms, broth, tomatoes, onion, bell peppers, wine, garlic, bay leaf, salt and black pepper to **CROCK-POT®** slow cooker. Add enough water to cover roast and vegetables. Cover; cook on LOW 4 to 6 hours. Remove and discard bay leaf before serving.

Makes 12 servings

Fantastic Pot Roast >

1   can (12 ounces) cola
1   bottle (10 ounces) chili sauce

2   cloves garlic
2½ pounds boneless beef chuck roast

Combine cola, chili sauce and garlic in **CROCK-POT**® slow cooker. Add beef; turn to coat. Cover; cook on LOW 6 to 8 hours. Serve with cooking liquid.

Makes 6 servings

Honey Ribs

2   pounds beef short ribs, trimmed
    and cut into 3- to 4-rib portions
1   can (about 14 ounces) beef broth
½   cup water
3   tablespoons soy sauce

2   tablespoons honey
2   tablespoons maple syrup
2   tablespoons barbecue sauce
½   teaspoon dry mustard
    Prepared corn (optional)

Combine ribs, broth, water, soy sauce, honey, syrup, barbecue sauce and mustard in **CROCK-POT**® slow cooker; stir to blend. Cover; cook on LOW 6 to 8 hours or on HIGH 4 to 6 hours. Serve with sauce and corn, if desired.

Makes 4 servings

Mini Puttanesca Meatballs >

1 package (about 1 pound) frozen cocktail-size beef meatballs

1 jar (24 to 26 ounces) marinara sauce

1/2 cup coarsely chopped pitted kalamata olives

2 tablespoons drained capers

1/2 to 3/4 teaspoon red pepper flakes
   Hot cooked spaghetti (optional)

1/4 cup chopped fresh basil or Italian parsley (optional)

Coat inside of **CROCK-POT**® slow cooker with nonstick cooking spray. Combine meatballs, marinara sauce, olives, capers and red pepper flakes in **CROCK-POT**® slow cooker. Cover; cook on LOW 3 to 4 hours or on HIGH 1 1/2 to 2 hours. Serve sauce and meatballs with spaghetti, if desired. Garnish with basil.

Makes 8 servings

Classic Chili

3 cans (about 15 ounces *each*) dark red kidney beans, rinsed and drained

2 cans (about 15 ounces *each*) tomato sauce

1 1/2 pounds ground beef, cooked and drained

1 1/2 cups chopped onion

1 can (about 14 ounces) diced tomatoes

1 cup chopped green bell pepper

2 cloves garlic, minced

2 to 3 teaspoons chili powder

1 to 2 teaspoons ground mustard

3/4 teaspoon dried basil

1/2 teaspoon black pepper

Combine beans, tomato sauce, beef, onion, tomatoes, bell pepper, garlic, chili powder, ground mustard, basil and black pepper in **CROCK-POT**® slow cooker; stir to blend. Cover; cook on LOW 8 to 10 hours or on HIGH 4 to 5 hours.

Makes 6 servings

Sweet and Sour Brisket Stew >

- 1 beef brisket (about 1 1/2 pounds), trimmed and cut into 1-inch cubes
- 1 jar (12 ounces) chili sauce
- 2 carrots, cut into 1/2-inch slices
- 1 onion, chopped
- 1/4 cup beef broth
- 1 1/2 tablespoons packed dark brown sugar
- 1 1/2 tablespoons lemon juice
- 1 tablespoon Dijon mustard
- 1 clove garlic, minced
- 1/4 teaspoon paprika
- 1/2 teaspoon salt
- 1/4 teaspoon black pepper

Combine beef, chili sauce, carrots, onion, broth, brown sugar, lemon juice, mustard, garlic, paprika, salt and pepper in **CROCK-POT**® slow cooker; stir to blend. Cover; cook on LOW 8 hours.

Makes 6 to 8 servings

Garlic and Mushroom Roast with Savory Gravy

- 1 (3- to 4-pound) beef roast
- 1 to 2 jars (12 ounces *each*) beef gravy
- 1 to 2 cans (4 ounces *each*) mushrooms, drained
- 1 medium onion, thinly sliced
- 3 large cloves garlic, sliced
  Salt and black pepper
  Hot cooked rice or couscous (optional)
  Chopped fresh Italian parsley (optional)

Combine roast, gravy, mushrooms, onion, garlic, salt and pepper in **CROCK-POT**® slow cooker; stir to blend. Cover; cook on LOW 8 to 10 hours. Serve over rice, if desired. Garnish with parsley.

Makes 8 to 10 servings

Ginger Beef with Peppers and Mushrooms

1½ pounds boneless beef top round
    steak, cut into ¾-inch cubes
24 baby carrots
1 onion, chopped
1 red bell pepper, chopped
1 green bell pepper, chopped
1 package (8 ounces) mushrooms,
    cut into halves

1 cup beef broth
½ cup hoisin sauce
¼ cup quick-cooking tapioca
2 tablespoons grated fresh ginger
    Hot cooked rice (optional)

Combine beef, carrots, onion, bell peppers, mushrooms, broth, hoisin sauce, tapioca and ginger in **CROCK-POT®** slow cooker. Cover; cook on LOW 8 to 9 hours. Serve over rice, if desired.

Makes 6 servings

✤ Tip

Boneless beef top round steak can also sometimes be found in the meat section packaged as London Broil. Both are the same cut of beef, however, London Broil is thicker.

Maple-Glazed Meatballs

2 packages (about 16 ounces *each*) frozen fully cooked meatballs, partially thawed and separated

1 can (20 ounces) pineapple chunks in juice, drained

1 1/2 cups ketchup

1 cup maple syrup

1/3 cup soy sauce

1 tablespoon quick-cooking tapioca

1 1/2 teaspoons ground allspice

1 teaspoon dry mustard

Hot cooked rice (optional)

Combine meatballs, pineapple, ketchup, maple syrup, soy sauce, tapioca, allspice and dry mustard in **CROCK-POT**® slow cooker; stir to blend. Cover; cook on LOW 5 to 6 hours. Serve over rice, if desired.

Makes about 48 meatballs

Yankee Pot Roast and Vegetables

3 medium baking potatoes (about
   1 pound), cut into quarters

2 large carrots, cut into $^3/_4$-inch
   slices

2 stalks celery, cut into $^3/_4$-inch slices

1 medium onion, sliced

1 large parsnip, cut into $^3/_4$-inch
   slices

2 whole bay leaves

1 teaspoon dried rosemary

$^1/_2$ teaspoon dried thyme

1 beef chuck pot roast (about
   $2^1/_2$ pounds), trimmed and
   cut into 1-inch pieces

   Salt and black pepper

$^1/_2$ cup beef broth

Combine potatoes, carrots, celery, onion, parsnip, bay leaves, rosemary and thyme in **CROCK-POT**® slow cooker. Place beef over vegetables; season with salt and pepper. Pour broth over beef. Cover; cook on LOW 8½ to 9 hours. Remove and discard bay leaves before serving.

Makes 10 to 12 servings

❖ Tip

*To make gravy, turn off the heat to the **CROCK-POT**® slow cooker after removing the meat and vegetables. Let cooking liquid stand 5 minutes. Skim off and discard fat. Turn the **CROCK-POT**® slow cooker to HIGH. For each cup of cooking liquid, stir $^1/_4$ cup cold water into 2 tablespoons all-purpose flour in small bowl until smooth. Whisk into **CROCK-POT**® slow cooker. Cover; cook on HIGH 15 minutes or until thickened.*

Easy Beef Burgundy >

1 1/2 pounds cubed beef stew meat
1 can (10 3/4 ounces) condensed cream of mushroom soup, undiluted
1 cup dry red wine
1 onion, chopped
1 can (4 ounces) sliced mushrooms, drained
1 package (about 1 ounce) dry onion soup mix
1 tablespoon minced garlic
   Hot cooked noodles (optional)

Combine beef, soup, wine, onion, mushrooms, soup mix and garlic in **CROCK-POT**® slow cooker. Cover; cook on LOW 6 to 8 hours. Serve over noodles, if desired.

Makes 4 to 6 servings

Swiss Steak

1 onion, sliced
1 clove garlic, minced
1 beef round steak (about 2 pounds), cut into 8 pieces and dusted with all-purpose flour, salt and black pepper
3 medium potatoes, unpeeled and diced
1 can (about 28 ounces) whole tomatoes, undrained
1 package (16 ounces) frozen peas and carrots
1 can (10 3/4 ounces) condensed tomato soup, undiluted
1 cup sliced celery

Combine onion and garlic in **CROCK-POT**® slow cooker. Add steak, potatoes, tomatoes, peas and carrots, soup and celery. Cover; cook on LOW 6 to 8 hours or on HIGH 3 to 4 hours.

Makes 8 servings

Slow-Cooked Beef Brisket Dinner

1 beef brisket (4 pounds), sliced into
   serving pieces
4 to 6 medium potatoes, cut into
   1-inch cubes
6 carrots, cut into 1-inch pieces
8 ounces mushrooms, sliced
½ large onion, sliced

1 stalk celery, cut into 1-inch pieces
3 cubes beef bouillon
5 cloves garlic, crushed
1 teaspoon black peppercorns
2 whole bay leaves
   Chopped fresh Italian parsley
   (optional)

Combine brisket, potatoes, carrots, mushrooms, onion, celery, bouillon cubes, garlic, peppercorns and bay leaves in **CROCK-POT**® slow cooker. Add enough water to cover ingredients. Cover; cook on LOW 3 to 4 hours. Remove and discard bay leaves. Serve beef with vegetables. Garnish with parsley.

Makes 8 to 10 servings

Asian Short Ribs >

3 pounds boneless beef short ribs
1/2 cup beef broth
1/4 cup dry sherry
1/4 cup soy sauce
1 tablespoon minced fresh ginger*
1 tablespoon honey
2 teaspoons minced garlic
1 teaspoon salt
1/2 teaspoon black pepper
   Hot cooked rice (optional)
1/2 cup chopped green onions
   (optional)

*To mince ginger quickly, cut a small chunk, remove the skin and put through a garlic press. Store remaining unpeeled ginger in a resealable food storage bag in the refrigerator up to 3 weeks.

Combine ribs, broth, sherry, soy sauce, ginger, honey, garlic, salt and pepper in **CROCK-POT®** slow cooker. Cover; cook on LOW 7 to 8 hours. Serve over rice, if desired. Garnish with green onions.

Makes 4 to 6 servings

Cajun Pot Roast

1 (3-pound) boneless beef chuck
   roast
1 can (about 14 ounces) diced
   tomatoes
1 can (about 14 ounces) diced
   tomatoes with mild green chiles
1 medium onion, chopped
1 cup *each* chopped rutabaga,
   mushrooms, turnip, parsnip and
   green bell pepper
1 cup green beans
1 cup sliced carrots
1 cup corn
3/4 cup water
2 tablespoons hot pepper sauce
1 to 2 tablespoons Cajun seasoning
1 teaspoon sugar
1/2 teaspoon black pepper

Combine beef, tomatoes, onion, rutabaga, mushrooms, turnip, parsnip, bell pepper, green beans, carrots, corn, water, hot pepper sauce, Cajun seasoning, sugar and black pepper in **CROCK-POT®** slow cooker; stir to blend. Cover; cook on LOW 6 hours.

Makes 6 servings

Party Meatballs >

1 package (about 1 pound) frozen cocktail-size beef meatballs
1/2 cup maple syrup
1 jar (12 ounces) chili sauce
1 jar (12 ounces) grape jelly
Hot cooked rice (optional)

Combine meatballs, syrup, chili sauce and jelly in **CROCK-POT**® slow cooker; stir to blend. Cover; cook on LOW 3 to 4 hours or on HIGH 2 to 3 hours. Serve over rice, if desired.

Makes 10 to 12 servings

Steak San Marino

1 beef round steak (about 1 1/2 pounds), cut into 4 pieces and dusted with all-purpose flour, salt and black pepper
1 can (8 ounces) tomato sauce
2 carrots, chopped
1/2 onion, chopped
1 stalk celery, chopped
1 teaspoon Italian seasoning
1/2 teaspoon Worcestershire sauce
1 whole bay leaf
Hot cooked rice (optional)

Place steak in **CROCK-POT**® slow cooker. Add tomato sauce, carrots, onion, celery, Italian seasoning, Worcestershire sauce and bay leaf. Cover; cook on LOW 8 to 10 hours or on HIGH 4 to 5 hours. Remove and discard bay leaf. Serve steaks and sauce over rice, if desired.

Makes 4 servings

Wild Mushroom Beef Stew

1½ to 2 pounds cubed beef stew meat
1½ cups beef broth
  4 shiitake mushrooms, sliced
  2 medium carrots, sliced
  2 medium potatoes, diced
  1 small white onion, chopped
  1 stalk celery, sliced

2 tablespoons all-purpose flour
½ teaspoon salt
½ teaspoon black pepper
1 teaspoon paprika
1 clove garlic, minced
1 teaspoon Worcestershire sauce
1 whole bay leaf

Combine beef, broth, mushrooms, carrots, potatoes, onion, celery, flour, salt, pepper, paprika, garlic, Worcestershire sauce and bay leaf in **CROCK-POT**® slow cooker; stir to blend. Cover; cook on LOW 10 to 12 hours or on HIGH 4 to 6 hours. Remove and discard bay leaf before serving.

Makes 5 servings

Note: This classic beef stew is given a twist with the addition of flavorful shiitake mushrooms. If shiitake mushrooms are unavailable in your local grocery store, you can substitute other mushrooms of your choice. For extra punch, add a few dried porcini mushrooms.

Portuguese Madeira Beef Shanks

4 medium beef shanks, bone in (about 3 pounds total)

1 cup beef broth

1 cup dry Madeira wine

1 large white onion, diced

1 green bell pepper, diced

1/2 cup diced celery

1/2 cup minced fresh Italian parsley

2 jalapeño peppers, seeded and minced*

4 cloves garlic, minced

1 tablespoon fresh rosemary, minced

1 teaspoon salt

Hot cooked rice (optional)

*Jalapeño peppers can sting and irritate the skin, so wear rubber gloves when handling peppers and do not touch your eyes.

Combine beef shanks, broth, wine, onion, bell pepper, celery, parsley, jalapeño peppers, garlic, rosemary and salt in **CROCK-POT**® slow cooker. Cover; cook on LOW 7 to 9 hours. Serve over rice, if desired, topped with sauce.

Makes 4 servings

Peppered Beef Tips >

1 **pound beef round tip roast or round steak, cut into 1- to 1½-inch cubes**

1 **can (10¾ ounces) condensed French onion soup, undiluted**

1 **can (10¾ ounces) condensed cream of mushroom soup, undiluted**

2 **cloves garlic, minced**

Black pepper

Hot cooked rice or noodles (optional)

Combine beef, soups, garlic and pepper in **CROCK-POT**® slow cooker. Cover; cook on LOW 8 to 10 hours. Serve over rice, if desired.

Makes 2 to 3 servings

Slow-Cooked Moroccan Dinner

1 **(4- to 5-pound) boneless beef chuck roast**

2 **medium potatoes, sliced**

2 **large onions, sliced**

2 **cups water**

1 **can (about 14 ounces) diced tomatoes**

1 **cup sliced carrots**

½ **cup chopped celery**

½ **cup dry chickpeas, rinsed and sorted**

½ **cup dry lentils, rinsed and sorted**

¼ **cup dates**

5 **cloves garlic, sliced**

1 **jalapeño pepper, minced***

2 **teaspoons** *each* **ground turmeric and ground ginger**

½ **teaspoon** *each* **ground cinnamon and ground red pepper**

Salt and black pepper

*Jalapeño peppers can sting and irritate the skin, so wear rubber gloves when handling peppers and do not touch your eyes.

Combine beef, potatoes, onions, water, tomatoes, carrots, celery, chickpeas, lentils, dates, garlic, jalapeño pepper, turmeric, ginger, cinnamon, ground red pepper, salt and black pepper in **CROCK-POT**® slow cooker; stir to blend. Cover; cook on LOW 8 hours.

Makes 6 servings

Ranch Stew

2 pounds cubed beef stew meat	2 tablespoons tapioca
6 medium potatoes, diced	1 tablespoon Worcestershire sauce
2 cups sliced carrots	2 teaspoons salt
2 medium onions, chopped	1 teaspoon soy sauce
1 can (10³/₄ ounces) condensed tomato soup, undiluted	¹/₄ teaspoon black pepper
1 soup can water	1 whole bay leaf

Combine beef, potatoes, carrots, onions, soup, water, tapioca, Worcestershire sauce, salt, soy sauce, pepper and bay leaf in **CROCK-POT**® slow cooker; stir to blend. Cover; cook on LOW 10 to 12 hours or on HIGH 5 to 6 hours. Remove and discard bay leaf.

Makes 6 servings

✤ Tip

*Vegetables, such as potatoes and carrots, can sometimes take longer to cook in a **CROCK-POT**® slow cooker compared with meat. Be sure to evenly place cut vegetables on the bottom or along the sides of the **CROCK-POT**® slow cooker when possible.*

MEATLESS MEALS

Summer Vegetable Stew

- 1 cup vegetable broth
- 1 can (about 15 ounces) chickpeas, rinsed and drained
- 1 medium zucchini, cut into 1/2-inch pieces
- 1 summer squash, cut into 1/2-inch pieces
- 4 large plum tomatoes, cut into 1/2-inch pieces
- 1 cup frozen corn
- 1/2 to 1 teaspoon dried rosemary
- 1/4 cup grated Asiago or Parmesan cheese (optional)
- 1 tablespoon chopped fresh Italian parsley (optional)

Combine broth, chickpeas, zucchini, squash, tomatoes, corn and rosemary in **CROCK-POT®** slow cooker; stir to blend. Cover; cook on LOW 8 hours or on HIGH 5 hours. Top each serving with cheese and parsley, if desired.

Makes 4 servings

Corn and Two Bean Chili

1 can (about 15 ounces) pinto or
  kidney beans, rinsed and drained
1 can (about 15 ounces) black beans,
  rinsed and drained
1 can (about 14 ounces) fire-roasted
  diced tomatoes
1 cup salsa

1 cup frozen corn
½ cup minced onion
1 teaspoon chili powder
1 teaspoon ground cumin
½ cup sour cream (optional)
1 cup (4 ounces) shredded Cheddar
  cheese (optional)

Coat inside of **CROCK-POT**® slow cooker with nonstick cooking spray. Combine beans, tomatoes, salsa, corn, onion, chili powder and cumin in **CROCK-POT**® slow cooker; stir to blend. Cover; cook on LOW 5 to 6 hours or on HIGH 2½ to 3 hours. Top each serving with sour cream and cheese, if desired.

Makes 4 servings

❖ Tip

Coating the inside of the **CROCK-POT**® *slow cooker with nonstick cooking spray makes cleanup easier.*

Artichoke Pasta Sauce>

1 can (about 28 ounces) crushed tomatoes
1 can (about 14 ounces) artichoke hearts, drained and chopped
1 cup chopped sweet onion
1 cup small pimiento-stuffed olives
4 cloves garlic, minced
$3/4$ teaspoon red pepper flakes
Hot cooked fettuccine pasta (optional)
$1/2$ cup grated Asiago or Romano cheese (optional)
Fresh basil leaves (optional)

Coat inside of **CROCK-POT**® slow cooker with nonstick cooking spray. Combine tomatoes, artichokes, onion, olives, garlic and red pepper flakes in **CROCK-POT**® slow cooker. Cover; cook on LOW 7 to 8 hours or on HIGH 3 to 4 hours. Serve over pasta, if desired. Garnish with cheese and basil.

Makes 4 servings

Creamy Red Pepper Polenta

6 cups boiling water
2 cups yellow cornmeal
1 small red bell pepper, finely chopped
$1/4$ cup ($1/2$ stick) butter, melted
2 teaspoons salt
$1/4$ teaspoon paprika, plus additional for garnish
$1/8$ teaspoon ground red pepper
$1/8$ teaspoon ground cumin

Combine water, cornmeal, bell pepper, butter, salt, $1/4$ teaspoon paprika, ground red pepper and cumin in **CROCK-POT**® slow cooker; stir to blend. Cover; cook on LOW 3 to 4 hours or on HIGH 1 to 2 hours. Garnish with additional paprika.

Makes 4 to 6 servings

Mushroom Barley Stew

2 containers (32 ounces *each*) vegetable broth

1 package (8 ounces) mushrooms, such as cremini, rinsed and thinly sliced

1 cup dried mushrooms, such as porcini, soaked in warm water to soften, liquid reserved

1 cup uncooked pearl barley, rinsed and sorted

2 carrots, diced

2 stalks celery, diced

1 yellow onion, diced

1 tablespoon fresh thyme

1 tablespoon tomato paste

2 whole bay leaves
   Salt and black pepper

2 tablespoons minced fresh Italian parsley (optional)

Combine broth, mushrooms, reserved mushroom liquid (taking care to discard any grit), barley, carrots, celery, onion, thyme, tomato paste, bay leaves, salt and black pepper in **CROCK-POT®** slow cooker. Cover; cook on LOW 5½ hours or on HIGH 3 to 4 hours. Remove and discard bay leaves. Garnish each serving with parsley.

Makes 8 servings

Vegetable Curry

4 baking potatoes, diced	**2 carrots, diced**
3 cups cauliflower florets	**1 can (6 ounces) tomato paste**
1 package (10 ounces) frozen peas	**1/2 cup water**
1 large onion, chopped	**2 teaspoons cumin seeds**
1 red bell pepper, chopped	**1/2 teaspoon garlic powder**
2 tomatoes, chopped	**1/2 teaspoon salt**

Combine potatoes, cauliflower, peas, onion, bell pepper, tomatoes, carrots, tomato paste, water, cumin seeds, garlic powder and salt in **CROCK-POT®** slow cooker; stir to blend. Cover; cook on LOW 8 to 10 hours.

Makes 6 servings

✤ Tip

If you are short on time, this recipe can also be cooked on HIGH 4 to 5 hours. One hour of slow cooking on HIGH equals two hours on LOW.

Macaroni and Cheese >

6 cups cooked elbow macaroni

6 cups (24 ounces) shredded
   Cheddar cheese

4 cups evaporated milk

2 tablespoons butter

2 teaspoons salt

1/2 teaspoon black pepper

Combine macaroni, cheese, evaporated milk, butter, salt and pepper in **CROCK-POT®** slow cooker. Cover; cook on HIGH 2 to 3 hours.

Makes 6 to 8 servings

Variations: Add some tasty mix-ins like diced green or red bell pepper, peas, chopped tomato or chopped onion.

Caribbean Sweet Potato and Bean Stew

2 sweet potatoes (about 1 pound),
   cut into 1-inch cubes

2 cups frozen cut green beans

1 can (about 15 ounces) black beans,
   rinsed and drained

1 can (about 14 ounces) vegetable
   broth

1 onion, sliced

2 teaspoons Caribbean jerk
   seasoning

1/2 teaspoon dried thyme

1/4 teaspoon salt

1/4 teaspoon ground cinnamon

1/3 cup slivered almonds, toasted
   (optional)*

*To toast almonds, spread in a single layer in heavy skillet. Cook over medium heat 1 to 2 minutes or until nuts are lightly browned, stirring frequently.

Combine sweet potatoes, beans, broth, onion, jerk seasoning, thyme, salt and cinnamon in **CROCK-POT®** slow cooker. Cover; cook on LOW 5 to 6 hours. Sprinkle with almonds, if desired.

Makes 4 servings

Vegetarian Chili

1 can (28 ounces) crushed tomatoes, undrained

1 can (about 15 ounces) black beans, rinsed and drained

1 can (about 15 ounces) chickpeas, rinsed and drained

1/2 cup corn

1/4 cup tomato paste

1 cup chopped onion

1 cup chopped red bell pepper

2 tablespoons minced jalapeño peppers*

1 clove garlic, minced

1 teaspoon sugar

1 teaspoon ground cumin

1 teaspoon dried basil

1 teaspoon chili powder

1/4 teaspoon black pepper

Sour cream and shredded Cheddar cheese (optional)

*Jalapeño peppers can sting and irritate the skin, so wear rubber gloves when handling peppers and do not touch your eyes.

Combine tomatoes, beans, chickpeas, corn, tomato paste, onion, bell pepper, jalapeño peppers, garlic, sugar, cumin, basil, chili powder and black pepper to **CROCK-POT®** slow cooker; stir to blend. Cover; cook on LOW 4 to 5 hours. Top with sour cream and cheese, if desired.

Makes 4 servings

Butternut Squash, Chickpea and Lentil Stew

2 cups peeled and diced butternut squash ($^1/_2$-inch pieces)

2 cups vegetable broth

1 can (about 15 ounces) chickpeas, rinsed and drained

1 can (about 14 ounces) fire-roasted diced tomatoes

1 cup chopped sweet onion

$^3/_4$ cup dried brown lentils, rinsed and sorted

2 teaspoons ground cumin or coriander

$^3/_4$ teaspoon salt

Sprigs fresh thyme (optional)

Coat inside of **CROCK-POT**® slow cooker with nonstick cooking spray. Combine squash, broth, chickpeas, tomatoes, onion, lentils, cumin and salt in **CROCK-POT**® slow cooker. Cover; cook on LOW 8 to 9 hours or on HIGH 4 to 4$^1/_2$ hours. Garnish each serving with thyme.

Makes 6 servings

Scalloped Tomatoes and Corn >

1 can (15 ounces) cream-style corn
1 can (about 14 ounces) diced tomatoes
3/4 cup saltine or soda cracker crumbs
1 egg, lightly beaten

2 teaspoons sugar
3/4 teaspoon black pepper
Chopped fresh tomatoes (optional)
Chopped fresh Italian parsley (optional)

Combine corn, diced tomatoes, cracker crumbs, egg, sugar and pepper in **CROCK-POT**® slow cooker; stir to blend. Cover; cook on LOW 4 to 6 hours. Sprinkle with fresh tomatoes and parsley before serving, if desired.

Makes 4 to 6 servings

No-Fuss Macaroni and Cheese

2 cups (about 8 ounces) uncooked elbow macaroni
1½ cups milk
4 ounces pasteurized process cheese product, cubed

1 cup (4 ounces) shredded mild Cheddar cheese
½ teaspoon salt
⅛ teaspoon black pepper

Combine macaroni, milk, cheese product, Cheddar cheese, salt and pepper in **CROCK-POT**® slow cooker; stir to blend. Cover; cook on LOW 2 to 3 hours.

Makes 6 to 8 servings

Quinoa and Vegetable Medley

2 medium sweet potatoes, cut into $\frac{1}{2}$-inch-thick slices

1 medium eggplant, cut into $\frac{1}{2}$-inch cubes

1 large green bell pepper, sliced

1 medium tomato, cut into wedges

2 cups vegetable broth

1 cup uncooked quinoa, rinsed and drained

1 small onion, cut into wedges

2 cloves garlic, minced

$\frac{1}{2}$ teaspoon salt

$\frac{1}{2}$ teaspoon dried thyme

$\frac{1}{4}$ teaspoon ground red pepper

$\frac{1}{4}$ teaspoon black pepper

$\frac{1}{4}$ teaspoon dried marjoram

Coat inside of **CROCK-POT®** slow cooker with nonstick cooking spray. Combine sweet potatoes, eggplant, bell pepper, tomato, broth, quinoa, onion, garlic, salt, thyme, ground red pepper, black pepper and marjoram in **CROCK-POT®** slow cooker; stir to blend. Cover; cook on LOW 5 hours or on HIGH 2$\frac{1}{2}$ hours.

Makes 6 servings

Chunky Vegetable Chili >

2 cans (about 15 ounces *each*) cannellini beans, rinsed and drained

1 cup frozen corn

1 cup water

1 onion, chopped

2 stalks celery, diced

1 can (6 ounces) tomato paste

1 can (4 ounces) diced mild green chiles, undrained

1 carrot, diced

3 cloves garlic, minced

1 tablespoon chili powder

2 teaspoons dried oregano

1/2 teaspoon salt

Fresh chopped cilantro (optional)

Combine beans, corn, water, onion, celery, tomato paste, chiles, carrot, garlic, chili powder, oregano and salt in **CROCK-POT®** slow cooker; stir to blend. Cover; cook on LOW 5 1/2 to 6 hours. Garnish each serving with cilantro.

Makes 6 servings

Artichoke and Tomato Paella

4 cups vegetable broth

2 cups converted white rice

1 can (13 3/4 ounces) artichoke hearts, quartered, rinsed and drained

5 ounces (1/2 of 10-ounce package) frozen chopped spinach, thawed and drained

1/2 cup frozen peas

1 medium green bell pepper, chopped

1 medium tomato, sliced into wedges

1 medium onion, chopped

1 medium carrot, chopped

3 cloves garlic, minced

1 tablespoon minced fresh Italian parsley

1/2 teaspoon black pepper

Combine broth, rice, artichokes, spinach, peas, bell pepper, tomato, onion, carrot, garlic, parsley and black pepper in **CROCK-POT®** slow cooker. Cover; cook on LOW 4 hours or on HIGH 2 hours.

Makes 8 servings

Mediterranean Stew

1 medium butternut squash, cut into 1-inch cubes

2 cups unpeeled eggplant, cut into 1-inch cubes

2 cups sliced zucchini

1 can (about 15 ounces) chickpeas, rinsed and drained

1 package (10 ounces) frozen cut okra

1 cup chopped onion

1 can (8 ounces) tomato sauce

1 medium fresh tomato, chopped

1 medium carrot, sliced

1/2 cup vegetable broth

1/3 cup raisins

1 clove garlic, minced

1/2 teaspoon ground cumin

1/2 teaspoon ground turmeric

1/4 teaspoon ground red pepper

1/4 teaspoon paprika

1/4 teaspoon ground cinnamon

6 to 8 cups hot cooked couscous (optional)

Chopped fresh Italian parsley (optional)

Combine squash, eggplant, zucchini, chickpeas, okra, onion, tomato sauce, fresh tomato, carrot, broth, raisins, garlic, cumin, turmeric, ground red pepper, paprika and cinnamon in **CROCK-POT®** slow cooker; stir to blend. Cover; cook on LOW 8 to 10 hours. Serve over couscous, if desired. Garnish with parsley.

Makes 6 servings

Vegetable Pasta Sauce

2 cans (about 14 ounces *each*) diced tomatoes

1 can (about 14 ounces) whole tomatoes, undrained

1½ cups sliced mushrooms

1 medium red bell pepper, diced

1 medium green bell pepper, diced

1 small yellow squash, cut into ¼-inch slices

1 small zucchini, cut into ¼-inch slices

1 can (6 ounces) tomato paste

4 green onions, sliced

2 tablespoons Italian seasoning

1 tablespoon chopped fresh Italian parsley

3 cloves garlic, minced

1 teaspoon salt

1 teaspoon red pepper flakes (optional)

1 teaspoon black pepper

Hot cooked rigatoni pasta (optional)

Grated Parmesan cheese (optional)

Combine tomatoes, mushrooms, bell peppers, squash, zucchini, tomato paste, green onions, Italian seasoning, parsley, garlic, salt, red pepper flakes, if desired, and black pepper in **CROCK-POT®** slow cooker; stir to blend. Cover; cook on LOW 6 to 8 hours. Serve over pasta, if desired. Top with cheese, if desired.

Makes 4 to 6 servings

Double-Hearty, Double-Quick Veggie Chili

2 cans (about 15 ounces *each*) dark
  kidney beans, rinsed and drained
2 bell peppers, chopped
1 can (about 14 ounces) diced
  tomatoes with peppers, celery
  and onions

1 cup frozen corn
3 tablespoons chili powder
2 teaspoons sugar
2 teaspoons ground cumin
  Sour cream (optional)
  Chopped fresh cilantro (optional)

Combine beans, bell peppers, tomatoes, corn, chili powder, sugar and cumin in
CROCK-POT® slow cooker; stir to blend. Cover; cook on LOW 5 hours or on HIGH
3 hours. Top with sour cream and cilantro, if desired.

Makes 4 servings

Hearty Vegetable and Potato Chowder >

2 cups vegetable broth
1 can (10³/₄ ounces) condensed cream of mushroom soup
1 package (10 ounces) frozen mixed vegetables (corn, carrots, peas and green beans)

2 medium russet potatoes (about 1 pound), cut into ¹/₂-inch cubes
2 to 3 teaspoons minced garlic
1¹/₂ teaspoons dried thyme
¹/₂ teaspoon black pepper

Coat inside of **CROCK-POT**® slow cooker with nonstick cooking spray. Add broth, soup, mixed vegetables, potatoes, garlic, thyme and pepper to **CROCK-POT**® slow cooker; stir to blend. Cover; cook on LOW 7 to 8 hours or on HIGH 3 to 4 hours.

Makes 6 servings

Cheesy Slow Cooker Potatoes

1 bag (32 ounces) shredded hash brown potatoes
2 cans (10¹/₂ ounces *each*) condensed Cheddar cheese soup, undiluted

1 can (12 ounces) evaporated milk
1 cup chopped onion

Combine potatoes, soup, evaporated milk and onion in **CROCK-POT**® slow cooker. Cover; cook on LOW 6 to 8 hours.

Makes 6 servings

Vegetable-Bean Pasta Sauce

- 2 cans (about 15 ounces *each*) cannellini beans, rinsed and drained
- 2 cans (about 14 ounces *each*) diced tomatoes
- 16 baby carrots
- 1 medium onion, sliced
- 1 can (6 ounces) tomato paste
- 1 ounce dried oyster mushrooms, chopped
- 1/4 cup grated Parmesan cheese
- 2 teaspoons garlic powder
- 1 teaspoon dried basil
- 1 teaspoon dried oregano
- 1/2 teaspoon dried rosemary
- 1/2 teaspoon dried marjoram
- 1/2 teaspoon dried sage
- 1/2 teaspoon dried thyme
- 1/4 teaspoon black pepper
- 1 package (12 ounces) whole wheat spaghetti noodles, cooked and drained (optional)

Combine beans, tomatoes, carrots, onion, tomato paste, mushrooms, cheese, garlic powder, basil, oregano, rosemary, marjoram, sage, thyme and pepper in **CROCK-POT®** slow cooker; stir to blend. Cover; cook on LOW 8 to 10 hours. Serve over noodles, if desired.

Makes 8 servings

Slow Cooker Veggie Stew >

2 cans (about 14 ounces *each*) vegetable broth
1 1/2 cups chopped green cabbage
2/3 cup carrot slices
1/2 cup diced onion
1/2 cup diced zucchini

1/2 cup cut green beans
1 tablespoon tomato paste
2 cloves garlic, chopped
1/2 teaspoon dried basil
1/2 teaspoon dried oregano
1/4 teaspoon salt

Combine broth, cabbage, carrots, onion, zucchini, green beans, tomato paste, garlic, basil, oregano and salt in **CROCK-POT®** slow cooker; stir to blend. Cover; cook on LOW 8 to 10 hours or on HIGH 4 to 5 hours.

Makes 4 to 6 servings

Southwestern Corn and Beans

2 cans (about 15 ounces *each*) kidney beans, rinsed and drained
1 bag (16 ounces) frozen corn
1 can (about 14 ounces) diced tomatoes
1 green bell pepper, cut into 1-inch pieces
1 large onion, chopped
1 or 2 jalapeño peppers, diced*

1 clove garlic, minced
2 teaspoons chili powder
1/2 teaspoon salt
1/2 teaspoon ground cumin
1/2 teaspoon black pepper
Sour cream (optional)
Sliced black olives (optional)

*Jalapeño peppers can sting and irritate the skin, so wear rubber gloves when handling peppers and do not touch your eyes.

Combine beans, corn, tomatoes, bell pepper, onion, jalapeño peppers, garlic, chili powder, salt, cumin and black pepper in **CROCK-POT®** slow cooker; stir to blend. Cover; cook on LOW 7 to 8 hours or on HIGH 2 to 3 hours. Serve with sour cream and black olives, if desired.

Makes 6 servings

Serving Suggestion: Spoon this colorful vegetarian dish into hollowed-out bell peppers.

Three-Bean Chipotle Chili

2 cans (about 15 ounces *each*) pinto or pink beans, rinsed and drained

1 can (about 15 ounces) small white beans, rinsed and drained

1 can (about 15 ounces) chickpeas, rinsed and drained

1 cup frozen corn

1 onion, chopped

1 green bell pepper, chopped

1 cup water

1 can (6 ounces) tomato paste

1 or 2 canned chipotle peppers in adobo sauce, finely chopped*

2 cloves garlic, minced

Salt and black pepper

Optional toppings: sour cream and shredded Cheddar cheese (optional)

Jalapeño peppers can sting and irritate the skin, so wear rubber gloves when handling peppers and do not touch your eyes.

Combine beans, chickpeas, corn, onion, bell pepper, water, tomato paste, chipotle peppers, garlic, salt and black pepper in **CROCK-POT®** slow cooker; stir to blend. Cover; cook on LOW 3½ to 4 hours. Top as desired.

Makes 6 servings

Garden Pasta >

- 1 jar (24 to 26 ounces) puttanesca or spicy tomato basil pasta sauce
- 1 can (about 14 ounces) stewed tomatoes
- 1 cup small broccoli florets
- 1 cup finely diced yellow squash or zucchini
- 2 cups (5 ounces) uncooked bowtie pasta
- 1/2 cup water
- 1/2 cup crumbled feta cheese (optional)
- 1/4 cup chopped fresh basil (optional)

Coat inside of **CROCK-POT**® slow cooker with nonstick cooking spray. Combine pasta sauce, tomatoes, broccoli, squash, pasta and water in **CROCK-POT**® slow cooker; stir to blend. Cover; cook on LOW 3$\frac{1}{2}$ to 4$\frac{1}{2}$ hours or on HIGH 2 to 2$\frac{1}{2}$ hours. Top with cheese and basil, if desired.

Makes 4 to 6 servings

Sweet-Sour Cabbage with Apples and Caraway Seeds

- 4 cups shredded red cabbage
- 1 large tart apple, peeled and cut crosswise into 1/4-inch-thick slices
- 1/4 cup packed light brown sugar
- 1/4 cup water
- 1/4 cup cider vinegar
- 1/2 teaspoon salt
- 1/4 teaspoon caraway seeds
  Dash black pepper

Combine cabbage, apple, brown sugar, water, vinegar, salt, caraway seeds and pepper in **CROCK-POT**® slow cooker. Cover; cook on LOW 2$\frac{1}{2}$ to 3 hours.

Makes 6 servings

Jamaican Quinoa and Sweet Potato Stew

3 cups vegetable broth

1 large or 2 small sweet potatoes (12 ounces), cut into ³/₄-inch pieces

1 cup uncooked quinoa, rinsed and drained

1 large red bell pepper, cut into ³/₄-inch pieces

1 tablespoon Caribbean jerk seasoning

¹/₄ cup chopped fresh cilantro (optional)

¹/₄ cup sliced almonds, toasted* (optional)

To toast almonds, spread in single layer in heavy skillet. Cook over medium heat 1 to 2 minutes or until nuts are lightly browned, stirring frequently.

Coat inside of **CROCK-POT**® slow cooker with nonstick cooking spray. Combine broth, sweet potatoes, quinoa, bell pepper and jerk seasoning in **CROCK-POT**® slow cooker. Cover; cook on LOW 5 to 6 hours or on HIGH 2 to 2¹/₂ hours. Top with cilantro and almonds, if desired.

Makes 4 servings

❖ Tip

Quinoa is a tiny round whole grain. It is higher in protein than other grains including wheat.

Wild Rice with Fruit

 5 cups chicken broth
 2 cups uncooked wild rice, rinsed*
 1 cup orange juice
 1/2 cup dried cranberries
 1/2 cup chopped raisins
 1/2 cup chopped dried apricots
 1/2 cup slivered almonds, toasted**
 2 tablespoons unsalted butter, melted

 1 teaspoon ground cumin
 2 green onions, thinly sliced (optional)
 2 tablespoons chopped fresh Italian parsley (optional)

*Do not use parboiled rice or a blend containing parboiled rice.

**To toast almonds, spread in single layer in heavy skillet. Cook and stir over medium heat 1 to 2 minutes or until nuts are lightly browned.

Combine broth, rice, orange juice, cranberries, raisins, apricots, almonds, butter and cumin in **CROCK-POT**® slow cooker; stir to blend. Cover; cook on LOW 7 hours or on HIGH 2 1/2 to 3 hours. Add green onions and parsley, if desired.

Makes 8 servings

Chili with Beans and Corn >

- 1 can (about 15 ounces) cannellini beans, rinsed and drained
- 1 can (about 15 ounces) kidney or navy beans, rinsed and drained
- 1 can (about 14 ounces) whole tomatoes, drained and chopped
- 1 onion, chopped
- 1 cup frozen corn
- 1 cup water

- 1/2 cup chopped green onions
- 1/2 cup tomato paste
- 1/4 cup diced jalapeño peppers*
- 1 tablespoon chili powder
- 1 teaspoon ground cumin
- 1 teaspoon prepared mustard
- 1/2 teaspoon dried oregano

Jalapeño peppers can sting and irritate the skin, so wear rubber gloves when handling peppers and do not touch your eyes.

Combine peas, beans, tomatoes, chopped onion, corn, water, green onions, tomato paste, jalapeño peppers, chili powder, cumin, mustard and oregano in **CROCK-POT®** slow cooker. Cover; cook on LOW 8 to 10 hours or on HIGH 4 to 5 hours.

Makes 6 to 8 servings

Three-Pepper Pasta Sauce

- 1 *each* red, yellow and green bell pepper, cut into 1-inch pieces
- 2 cans (about 14 ounces *each*) diced tomatoes
- 1 cup chopped onion
- 1 can (6 ounces) tomato paste
- 4 cloves garlic, minced
- 2 tablespoons olive oil

- 1 teaspoon dried basil
- 1 teaspoon dried oregano
- 1/2 teaspoon salt
- 1/4 teaspoon red pepper flakes or black pepper
- Hot cooked pasta (optional)
- Grated Parmesan or Romano cheese (optional)

Combine bell peppers, tomatoes, onion, tomato paste, garlic, oil, basil, oregano, salt and red pepper flakes in **CROCK-POT®** slow cooker. Cover; cook on LOW 7 to 8 hours. Serve over pasta, if desired. Garnish with cheese.

Makes 4 to 6 servings

SIDE
✤ DISHES ✤

Brussels Sprouts with Raisins, Bacon and Thyme >

2 pounds Brussels sprouts, trimmed and cut into quarters

1 cup chicken broth

$2/3$ cup golden raisins

2 thick slices applewood smoked bacon, chopped

2 tablespoons chopped fresh thyme

Combine Brussels sprouts, broth, raisins, bacon and thyme in **CROCK-POT**® slow cooker. Cover; cook on LOW 3 to 4 hours.

Makes 8 servings

Slow-Good Apples and Carrots

6 carrots, sliced into $1/2$-inch slices

4 apples, peeled and sliced

$1/4$ cup plus 1 tablespoon all-purpose flour

1 tablespoon packed brown sugar

$1/2$ teaspoon ground nutmeg

1 tablespoon butter, cubed

$1/2$ cup orange juice

Layer carrots and apples in **CROCK-POT**® slow cooker. Sprinkle with flour, brown sugar and nutmeg. Dot with butter; pour in juice. Cover; cook on LOW $31/2$ to 4 hours.

Makes 6 servings

Red Cabbage and Apples >

1 small head red cabbage, thinly sliced
1 large apple, peeled and grated
$^3/_4$ cup sugar
$^1/_2$ cup red wine vinegar

1 teaspoon ground cloves
$^1/_2$ cup bacon, crisp-cooked and crumbled (optional)
Fresh apple slices (optional)

Combine cabbage, grated apples, sugar, vinegar and cloves in **CROCK-POT®** slow cooker. Cover; cook on HIGH 6 hours. Sprinkle with bacon, if desired. Garnish with apple slices.

Makes 6 servings

Garden Potatoes

$1^1/_4$ pounds baking potatoes, sliced
1 small green or red bell pepper, thinly sliced
$^1/_4$ cup finely chopped yellow onion
2 tablespoons butter, divided
$^1/_2$ teaspoon salt

$^1/_2$ teaspoon dried thyme
Black pepper
1 small yellow squash, thinly sliced
1 cup (4 ounces) shredded sharp Cheddar cheese (optional)
Chopped fresh chives (optional)

Place potatoes, bell pepper, onion, 1 tablespoon butter, salt, thyme and black pepper in **CROCK-POT®** slow cooker. Evenly layer squash over potato mixture; add remaining 1 tablespoon butter. Cover; cook on LOW 7 hours or on HIGH 4 hours. Sprinkle with cheese and chives, if desired.

Makes 5 servings

Braised Beets with Cranberries >

2½ pounds medium beets, peeled and
    cut into 6 pieces

1 cup cranberry juice

½ cup sweetened dried cranberries

2 tablespoons quick-cooking tapioca

2 tablespoons butter, cut into small
    pieces

2 tablespoons honey

½ teaspoon salt

⅓ cup crumbled blue cheese
    (optional)

Orange peel, thinly sliced
    (optional)

Combine beets, cranberry juice, cranberries, tapioca, butter, honey and salt in **CROCK-POT®**
slow cooker; stir to blend. Cover; cook on LOW 7 to 8 hours. Garnish with blue cheese and
orange peel.

Makes 6 to 8 servings

Herbed Fall Vegetables

2 medium Yukon Gold potatoes, cut
    into ½-inch pieces

2 medium sweet potatoes, cut into
    ½-inch pieces

3 parsnips, cut into ½-inch pieces

1 medium bulb of fennel, sliced and
    cut into ½-inch pieces

1 cup chicken broth

¾ cup chopped fresh Italian parsley

2 tablespoons unsalted butter,
    cubed

1 tablespoon salt

½ teaspoon black pepper

Combine potatoes, parsnips, fennel, broth, parsley, butter, salt and pepper in
CROCK-POT® slow cooker. Cover; cook on LOW 4½ hours or on HIGH 3 hours.

Makes 6 servings

Orange Spiced Sweet Potatoes >

2 pounds sweet potatoes, diced
$\frac{1}{2}$ cup packed dark brown sugar
$\frac{1}{2}$ cup (1 stick) butter, cubed
1 teaspoon ground cinnamon
1 teaspoon vanilla
$\frac{1}{2}$ teaspoon salt
$\frac{1}{2}$ teaspoon ground nutmeg

$\frac{1}{2}$ teaspoon grated orange peel
Juice of 1 medium orange
Chopped toasted pecans (optional)*

To toast pecans, spread in single layer in small skillet. Cook and stir over medium heat 1 to 2 minutes or until nuts are lightly browned.

Combine sweet potatoes, brown sugar, butter, cinnamon, vanilla, salt, nutmeg, orange peel and orange juice in **CROCK-POT®** slow cooker. Cover; cook on LOW 4 hours or on HIGH 2 hours. Sprinkle with pecans, if desired.

Makes 8 servings

Mushroom Wild Rice

$1\frac{1}{2}$ cups chicken broth
1 cup uncooked wild rice
$\frac{1}{2}$ cup diced onion
$\frac{1}{2}$ cup sliced mushrooms

$\frac{1}{2}$ cup diced red or green bell pepper
1 tablespoon olive oil
$\frac{1}{4}$ teaspoon salt
$\frac{1}{4}$ teaspoon black pepper

Combine broth, rice, onion, mushrooms, bell pepper, oil, salt and black pepper in **CROCK-POT®** slow cooker; stir to blend. Cover; cook on HIGH $2\frac{1}{2}$ hours or until rice is tender and liquid is absorbed.

Makes 8 servings

Lemon and Tangerine Glazed Carrots >

6 cups sliced carrots
1½ cups apple juice
6 tablespoons butter
¼ cup packed brown sugar

2 tablespoons grated lemon peel
2 tablespoons grated tangerine peel
½ teaspoon salt
Chopped fresh Italian parsley

Combine carrots, apple juice, butter, brown sugar, lemon peel, tangerine peel and salt in **CROCK-POT®** slow cooker. Cover; cook on LOW 4 to 5 hours or on HIGH 1 to 3 hours. Garnish with parsley.

Makes 10 to 12 servings

Winter Squash and Apples

1 butternut squash (about 2 pounds), cut into 2-inch pieces
2 apples, sliced
1 medium onion, quartered and sliced

1 teaspoon salt
½ teaspoon black pepper, plus additional for seasoning
1½ tablespoons butter (optional)

Combine squash, apples, onion, salt and pepper in **CROCK-POT®** slow cooker; stir to blend. Cover; cook on LOW 6 to 7 hours. Stir in butter, if desired.

Makes 4 to 6 servings

Green Bean Casserole >

2 packages (10 ounces *each*) frozen green beans
1 can (10³/₄ ounces) condensed cream of mushroom soup, undiluted
1 tablespoon chopped fresh Italian parsley
1 tablespoon chopped roasted red peppers
1 teaspoon dried sage
¹/₂ teaspoon salt
¹/₂ teaspoon black pepper
¹/₄ teaspoon ground nutmeg
¹/₂ cup toasted slivered almonds (optional)*

To toast almonds, spread in single layer in small skillet. Cook and stir over medium heat 1 to 2 minutes or until nuts are lightly browned.

Combine green beans, soup, parsley, red peppers, sage, salt, black pepper and nutmeg in **CROCK-POT®** slow cooker; stir to blend. Cover; cook on LOW 3 to 4 hours. Sprinkle each serving with almonds, if desired.

Makes 6 servings

Candied Sweet Potatoes

3 medium sweet potatoes (1¹/₂ to 2 pounds), sliced into ¹/₂-inch rounds
¹/₂ cup water
¹/₄ cup (¹/₂ stick) butter, cut into pieces
2 tablespoons sugar
1 tablespoon vanilla
1 teaspoon ground nutmeg

Combine sweet potatoes, water, butter, sugar, vanilla and nutmeg in **CROCK-POT®** slow cooker; stir to blend. Cover; cook on LOW 7 hours or on HIGH 4 hours.

Makes 4 servings

Simmered Napa Cabbage with Dried Apricots >

4 cups napa cabbage or green cabbage, thinly sliced

1 cup chopped dried apricots

1/2 cup dry red wine

1/4 cup clover honey

2 tablespoons orange juice

Salt and black pepper

Grated orange peel (optional)

Combine cabbage, apricots, wine, honey, orange juice, salt and pepper in **CROCK-POT®** slow cooker; stir to blend. Cover; cook on LOW 5 to 6 hours or on HIGH 2 to 3 hours. Garnish with orange peel.

Makes 4 servings

Collard Greens

4 bunches collard greens, stemmed, washed and torn into 1-inch pieces

2 cups water

1/2 medium red bell pepper, cut into strips

1/3 medium green bell pepper, cut into strips

1/4 cup olive oil

1/4 teaspoon salt

1/4 teaspoon black pepper

Combine collard greens, water, bell peppers, oil, salt and black pepper in **CROCK-POT®** slow cooker; stir to blend. Cover; cook on LOW 3 to 4 hours or on HIGH 2 hours.

Makes 10 servings

Bacon and Cheese Brunch Potatoes >

3 medium russet potatoes (about 2 pounds), cut into 1-inch cubes

1 cup chopped onion

1/2 teaspoon seasoned salt

4 slices bacon, crisp-cooked and crumbled

1 cup (4 ounces) shredded sharp Cheddar cheese

1 tablespoon water

Coat inside of **CROCK-POT**® slow cooker with nonstick cooking spray. Place half of potatoes in **CROCK-POT**® slow cooker. Sprinkle half of onion and seasoned salt over potatoes; top with half of bacon and cheese. Repeat layers, ending with cheese. Sprinkle water over top. Cover; cook on LOW 6 hours or on HIGH 3 1/2 hours. Stir gently to mix; serve warm.

Makes 6 servings

Lentils with Carrots

3 cups chicken broth

1 cup dried brown lentils, rinsed and sorted

2 large carrots, chopped

1 small onion or large shallot, chopped

1 stalk celery, chopped

1/4 teaspoon dried thyme
Salt and black pepper

1/4 cup chopped walnuts (optional)*

*To toast walnuts, spread in single layer in small skillet. Cook and stir over medium heat 1 to 2 minutes or until nuts are lightly browned.

Combine broth, lentils, carrots, onion, celery, thyme, salt and pepper in **CROCK-POT**® slow cooker; stir to blend. Cover; cook on HIGH 3 hours. Sprinkle with walnuts, if desired.

Makes 4 to 6 servings

Tip: Lentils should absorb most or all of the broth. To check, slightly tilt the **CROCK-POT**® slow cooker without removing the lid.

SWEET
❧ TREATS ❧

3-Fruit Oatmeal

4¹⁄₄ cups water
1 cup steel-cut oats
¹⁄₃ cup golden raisins
¹⁄₃ cup dried cranberries
¹⁄₃ cup dried cherries

2 tablespoons honey
1 teaspoon vanilla
¹⁄₄ teaspoon salt
Sliced fresh strawberries (optional)

Combine water, oats, raisins, cranberries, cherries, honey, vanilla and salt in **CROCK-POT®** slow cooker; stir to blend. Cover; cook on LOW 7 to 7¹⁄₂ hours. Top each serving with strawberries, if desired.

Makes 4 servings

Cherry Delight >

1 can (21 ounces) cherry pie filling
1 package (about 18 ounces) yellow
  cake mix

$1/2$ cup (1 stick) butter, melted
$1/3$ cup chopped walnuts

Layer pie filling, cake mix, butter and walnuts in **CROCK-POT®** slow cooker. Cover; cook on LOW 3 to 4 hours or on HIGH $1/2$ to 2 hours.

Makes 8 to 10 servings

Spiced Apple and Cranberry Compote

$2^{1}/_{2}$ cups cranberry juice cocktail
1 package (6 ounces) dried apples
$1/2$ cup (2 ounces) dried cranberries
$1/2$ cup Rhine wine or apple juice
$1/2$ cup honey

2 cinnamon sticks, broken into
  halves
Frozen yogurt or ice cream
  (optional)

1. Combine juice, apples, cranberries, wine, honey and 4 cinnamon sticks in **CROCK-POT®** slow cooker. Cover; cook on LOW 4 to 5 hours or until liquid is absorbed and fruit is tender.

2. Remove and discard cinnamon sticks. Serve with yogurt, if desired.

Makes 6 servings

Hawaiian Fruit Compote

3 cups coarsely chopped fresh
   pineapple

3 grapefruits, peeled and sectioned

1 can (21 ounces) cherry pie filling

2 cups chopped fresh peaches

2 to 3 limes, peeled and sectioned

1 mango, peeled and chopped

2 bananas, sliced

1 tablespoon lemon juice
   Slivered almonds (optional)

Combine pineapple, grapefruits, pie filling, peaches, limes, mango, bananas and lemon juice in **CROCK-POT®** slow cooker; stir to blend. Cover; cook on LOW 4 to 5 hours or on HIGH 2 to 3 hours. Sprinkle with almonds, if desired.

Makes 8 servings

Serving Suggestions: Try warm, fruity compote in place of maple syrup on your favorite waffles or pancakes for a great way to start your day. This sauce is also delicious served over roasted turkey, pork roast or baked ham.

Figs Poached in Red Wine >

2 cups dry red wine	2 (3-inch) cinnamon sticks
1 cup packed brown sugar	1 teaspoon finely grated orange peel
12 dried Calimyrna or Mediterranean figs (about 6 ounces)	4 tablespoons whipping cream (optional)

1. Combine wine, brown sugar, figs, cinnamon sticks and orange peel in **CROCK-POT®** slow cooker. Cover; cook on LOW 5 to 6 hours or on HIGH 4 to 5 hours.

2. Remove and discard cinnamon sticks. To serve, spoon figs and syrup into serving dish. Top with spoonful of cream, if desired.

Makes 4 servings

Homestyle Apple Brown Betty

6 cups of your favorite cooking apples, peeled and cut into eighths	1/2 cup (1 stick) butter, melted
1 cup dry bread crumbs	1/4 cup finely chopped walnuts
3/4 cup packed brown sugar	1 teaspoon ground cinnamon
	1 teaspoon ground nutmeg
	1/8 teaspoon salt

Coat inside of **CROCK-POT®** slow cooker with nonstick cooking spray. Place apples on bottom. Top with bread crumbs, brown sugar, butter, walnuts, cinnamon, nutmeg and salt. Cover; cook on LOW 3 to 4 hours or on HIGH 2 hours.

Makes 8 servings

Cinnamon Roll-Topped Mixed Berry Cobbler >

- 2 bags (12 ounces *each*) frozen mixed berries
- 1 cup sugar
- 1/4 cup quick-cooking tapioca
- 1/4 cup water

- 2 teaspoons vanilla
- 1 package (about 12 ounces) refrigerated cinnamon rolls with icing

Combine berries, sugar, tapioca, water and vanilla in **CROCK-POT®** slow cooker; top with cinnamon rolls. Cover; cook on LOW 4 to 5 hours. Drizzle with icing, if desired.

Makes 8 servings

Note: Double the ingredients for larger **CROCK-POT®** slow cookers, but always place cinnamon rolls in a single layer.

Pear Crunch

- 1 can (8 ounces) crushed pineapple in juice, undrained
- 1/4 cup pineapple or apple juice
- 3 tablespoons dried cranberries
- 1 1/2 teaspoons quick-cooking tapioca

- 1/4 teaspoon vanilla
- 2 pears, cored and halved
- 1/4 cup granola with almonds (optional)

Combine pineapple, juice, cranberries, tapioca and vanilla in **CROCK-POT®** slow cooker; stir to blend. Top with pears, cut sides down. Cover; cook on LOW 3 1/2 to 4 1/2 hours. Sprinkle each serving with granola, if desired.

Makes 4 servings

"Peachy Keen" Dessert >

2 pounds fresh peaches (about
   8 medium), sliced
1 1/3 cups old-fashioned oats
1 cup granulated sugar

1 cup packed light brown sugar
2/3 cup buttermilk baking mix
2 teaspoons ground cinnamon
1/2 teaspoon ground nutmeg

Combine peaches, oats, granulated sugar, brown sugar, baking mix, cinnamon and nutmeg in **CROCK-POT**® slow cooker; stir to blend. Cover; cook on LOW 4 to 6 hours.

Makes 8 to 12 servings

Five-Spice Apple Crisp

3 tablespoons unsalted butter,
   melted
6 Golden Delicious apples, peeled
   and cut into 1/2-inch-thick slices
2 teaspoons lemon juice
1/4 cup packed brown sugar
3/4 teaspoon Chinese five-spice
   powder, plus additional for
   garnish

1 cup coarsely crushed Chinese-
   style almond cookies or almond
   biscotti (optional)
Sweetened whipped cream
   (optional)

Butter inside of **CROCK-POT**® slow cooker with melted butter. Add apples and lemon juice. Sprinkle apples with brown sugar and 3/4 teaspoon five-spice powder. Cover; cook on LOW 3 1/2 hours. Sprinkle cookies over apples, if desired. Garnish with whipped cream and additional five-spice powder.

Makes 4 servings

Pumpkin-Cranberry Custard >

1 can (30 ounces) pumpkin pie filling
1 can (12 ounces) evaporated milk
1 cup dried cranberries

4 eggs, beaten
1 cup whole or crushed gingersnap cookies (optional)

Combine pumpkin, evaporated milk, cranberries and eggs in **CROCK-POT**® slow cooker; stir to blend. Cover; cook on HIGH 4 to 4½ hours. Serve with gingersnaps, if desired.

Makes 4 to 6 servings

Cherry-Orange Oatmeal

4 cups water
2 cups old-fashioned oats
¼ cup sugar
2 tablespoons unsweetened cocoa powder

2 cups fresh pitted cherries or frozen dark sweet cherries (optional)
2 cans (11 ounces *each*) mandarin orange segments in light syrup, drained and rinsed (optional)

Combine water, oats, sugar and cocoa in **CROCK-POT**® slow cooker. Cover; cook on LOW 8 hours. Top each serving with cherries and oranges, if desired.

Makes 8 servings

Apple and Granola Breakfast Cobbler >

4 medium Granny Smith apples, peeled, cored and sliced

2 cups granola cereal, plus additional for garnish

1/2 cup packed light brown sugar

2 tablespoons butter, cubed

1 tablespoon lemon juice

1 teaspoon ground cinnamon
Whipping cream, half-and-half or yogurt (optional)

Place apples in **CROCK-POT**® slow cooker. Sprinkle with 2 cups granola, brown sugar, butter, lemon juice and cinnamon. Cover; cook on LOW 6 hours or on HIGH 2 to 3 hours. Garnish with additional granola and cream, if desired.

Makes 4 servings

Decadent Chocolate Delight

1 package (about 18 ounces) chocolate cake mix

1 container (8 ounces) sour cream

1 cup semisweet chocolate chips

1 cup water

4 eggs

1/2 cup vegetable oil

1 package (4-serving size) instant chocolate pudding and pie filling mix
Vanilla ice cream (optional)

Coat inside of **CROCK-POT**® slow cooker with nonstick cooking spray. Combine cake mix, sour cream, chocolate chips, water, eggs, oil and pie filling mix in **CROCK-POT**® slow cooker; stir to blend. Cover; cook on LOW 3 to 4 hours or on HIGH 1 1/2 to 1 3/4 hours. Serve with ice cream, if desired.

Makes 12 servings

INDEX 191

Metric Conversion Chart

VOLUME MEASUREMENTS (dry)

1/8 teaspoon = 0.5 mL
1/4 teaspoon = 1 mL
1/2 teaspoon = 2 mL
3/4 teaspoon = 4 mL
1 teaspoon = 5 mL
1 tablespoon = 15 mL
2 tablespoons = 30 mL
1/4 cup = 60 mL
1/3 cup = 75 mL
1/2 cup = 125 mL
2/3 cup = 150 mL
3/4 cup = 175 mL
1 cup = 250 mL
2 cups = 1 pint = 500 mL
3 cups = 750 mL
4 cups = 1 quart = 1 L

VOLUME MEASUREMENTS (fluid)

1 fluid ounce (2 tablespoons) = 30 mL
4 fluid ounces (1/2 cup) = 125 mL
8 fluid ounces (1 cup) = 250 mL
12 fluid ounces (1 1/2 cups) = 375 mL
16 fluid ounces (2 cups) = 500 mL

WEIGHTS (mass)

1/2 ounce = 15 g
1 ounce = 30 g
3 ounces = 90 g
4 ounces = 120 g
8 ounces = 225 g
10 ounces = 285 g
12 ounces = 360 g
16 ounces = 1 pound = 450 g

DIMENSIONS

1/16 inch = 2 mm
1/8 inch = 3 mm
1/4 inch = 6 mm
1/2 inch = 1.5 cm
3/4 inch = 2 cm
1 inch = 2.5 cm

OVEN TEMPERATURES

250°F = 120°C
275°F = 140°C
300°F = 150°C
325°F = 160°C
350°F = 180°C
375°F = 190°C
400°F = 200°C
425°F = 220°C
450°F = 230°C

BAKING PAN SIZES

Utensil	Size in Inches/Quarts	Metric Volume	Size in Centimeters
Baking or Cake Pan (square or rectangular)	8×8×2	2 L	20×20×5
	9×9×2	2.5 L	23×23×5
	12×8×2	3 L	30×20×5
	13×9×2	3.5 L	33×23×5
Loaf Pan	8×4×3	1.5 L	20×10×7
	9×5×3	2 L	23×13×7
Round Layer Cake Pan	8×1½	1.2 L	20×4
	9×1½	1.5 L	23×4
Pie Plate	8×1¼	750 mL	20×3
	9×1¼	1 L	23×3
Baking Dish or Casserole	1 quart	1 L	—
	1½ quart	1.5 L	—
	2 quart	2 L	—